OLD ENGLISH METRE: AN INTRODUCTION

Old English Metre offers an essential framework for the critical analysis of metrical structures and interpretations in Old English literature. Jun Terasawa's comprehensive introductory text covers the basics of Old English metre and reviews the current research in the field, emphasizing the interaction between Old English metre and components such as word-formation, word-choice, and grammar. He also covers the metre-related problems of dating, authorship, and the distinction between prose and verse.

Each chapter includes exercises and suggestions for further reading. Appendices provide possible answers to the exercises, tips for scanning half-lines, and brief definitions of metrical terms used. Examples in Old English are provided with literal modern English translations, with glosses added in the first three chapters to help beginners. The result is a comprehensive guide that makes important text-critical skills more readily available to Old English specialists and beginners alike.

(Toronto Anglo-Saxon Series)

JUN TERASAWA is a professor in the Graduate School of Arts and Sciences at the University of Tokyo.

JUN TERASAWA

Old English Metre: An Introduction

UNIVERSITY OF TORONTO PRESS
Toronto Buffalo London

Toronto Buffalo London
www.utppublishing.com
Printed in Canada
ISBN 978-1-4426-4238-6 (cloth)
ISBN 978-1-4426-1129-0 (paper)

♾

Printed on acid-free, 100% post-consumer recycled paper with vegetable-based inks.

Library and Archives Canada Cataloguing in Publication

Terasawa, Jun, 1959–
Old English metre : an introduction / Jun Terasawa.

(Toronto Anglo-Saxon series ; 7)
Includes bibliographical references and index.

ISBN 978-1-4426-4238-6 (bound). – ISBN 978-1-4426-1129-0 (pbk.)

1. English language – Old English, ca. 450–1100 – Metrics and rhythmics. I. Title. II. Series: Toronto Anglo-Saxon series ; 7

PE253.T47 2011 429'.16 C2010-905887-9

University of Toronto Press gratefully acknowledges the financial assistance of the Centre for Medieval Studies, University of Toronto, in the publication of this book.

University of Toronto Press acknowledges the financial assistance to its publishing program of the Canada Council for the Arts and the Ontario Arts Council.

Canada Council for the Arts Conseil des Arts du Canada
ONTARIO ARTS COUNCIL CONSEIL DES ARTS DE L'ONTARIO

University of Toronto Press acknowledges the financial support of the Government of Canada through the Canada Book Fund for its publishing activities.

Contents

Preface

'The lack of an elementary introduction to Old English metre has long been felt by teachers and by students alike,' wrote Alan Bliss in his preface to *An Introduction to Old English Metre* in 1962. Bliss's *Introduction* has long since served to meet the needs of teachers introducing Old English metre and of students studying the subject for the first time.

Since then, however, considerable advances have been made in the field of Old English metre. In particular, the last few decades have seen a flourishing revival of interest in Old English metrical studies. While the detailed statistical analyses by Bliss and his predecessor Eduard Sievers led to neat classifications of possible metrical patterns and pinpointed rarely attested patterns, attempts have recently been made to account for why the metre of Old English poetry should take the shape that Sievers and Bliss described, and why certain metrical patterns, whether alliterative or rhythmic, are almost consistently avoided in Old English (cf. Cable 1974, 1991; Russom 1987; Fujiwara 1990; Suzuki 1996a). Furthermore, with the help of a computerized database, a detailed description of Old English metre has been made possible on the basis of a much more extensive corpus than was available in Sievers's and Bliss's times (cf. Hutcheson 1995). A few metrists have attempted to challenge the fundamental principles of the Sievers-Bliss theories, such as stress/rhythm-based metre and the four-position principle (cf. Hoover 1985; Obst 1987).

Due to a growing interest in Old English syntax after Bruce Mitchell's monumental work (Mitchell 1985), much work has been done on Old English metre in relation to grammar and syntax. Hans Kuhn's observations about the placement of stressed and unstressed words in the verse clause (commonly known as Kuhn's Laws) have been tested against a more extensive corpus (cf. Momma 1997) while Sievers's rhythmic types of half-lines have been reinterpreted with regard to the positions they can occupy in a verse clause (cf. Kendall 1991). Nakagawa (1982) and Macrae-Gibson (1986) reinterpret Sievers-Bliss's rhythmic types according to their syntactic structures.

Metre interacts not only with grammar and syntax but also with word-formation or the word-choice made by the poets. Old English poets tend to avoid certain metrical sequences in compounds, certain inflected forms of a given word, and certain suffixes, for example. Word-formation in the poetry is highly constrained on metrical grounds (cf. Terasawa 1989, 1992, 1994, 2001, 2007a).

Much-discussed topics relevant to Old English metre have continued to attract scholarly attention, including problems of dating Old English verse texts (cf. Amos 1980; Chase 1981; Fulk 1992, 2007b; Hutcheson 2004; Frank 2007) and problems of authorship (cf. Donoghue 1987b; Momma 1997; Terasawa 2005). Old English metre has also been placed in a comparative perspective with Middle English metre, other Germanic metres, and non-Germanic metres (cf. Cable 1991; Whitman 1993; Russom 1998; Suzuki 2004).

Despite the recent developments in research on Old English metre outlined above, Bliss's *Introduction* has not been revised to reap their fruits although it was reprinted in 1993 as a Subsidia volume of the *Old English Newsletter*. With a handful of exceptions (cf. Cassidy and Ringler 1971; Pope-Fulk 2001; McCully and Hilles 2005; Baker 2007),[1] recent Old English grammar books and readers often dispense with metrical matters, or at best content themselves with a brief introduction to the subject. Thus, the need for a new introductory book on Old English metre might be felt by scholars, teachers, and students alike, just as when Bliss published his *Introduction*.

This book is intended to achieve a twofold purpose. First, as an introductory book, it attempts to provide beginners with the basics of Old English metre, which will be described primarily in chapters 1, 2, and 3. The gist of Old English metre can be obtained from chapter 1, the first section of chapter 2 ('Consonantal and Vocalic Alliteration'), and the first three sections of chapter 3 ('Stress-words, Particles, and Proclitics,' 'Syllable and Foot,' and 'Five Rhythmic Types'). Those who want to learn

1 Stockwell and Minkova (1997a) provide a convenient summary of the Sievers-Bliss theory along with alternative theories. Bredehoft (2005b) is the most recent introduction to Old English metre, which can help non-specialists to scan half-lines properly on the basis of Sievers-Bliss's, Russom's, and his own system.

more about alliteration and rhythm in Old English poetry should consult chapter 4 as well as the rest of chapters 2 and 3. Appendices B and C provide some tips for scanning half-lines and a brief definition of metrical terms used in the book respectively. Second, the book provides an up-to-date view of current work in the field of Old English metre. Greater emphasis on the interaction between Old English metre and other components, such as word-formation/word-choice (cf. chapter 5) and grammar (cf. chapter 6), will be one of the distinctive features of the work. New light will be shed on the metre-related problems of dating, authorship, and the distinction between verse and prose (cf. chapter 7).

Information that is useful but of secondary importance is relegated to small type that beginners may skip over at first reading. (Such information is labelled with a single star (★) if it is useful for intermediate students, and with double stars (★★) if useful for advanced students/scholars.) While Bliss's *Introduction* is in part an outline of his own theory, this work, following the Sievers-Bliss tradition in principle, draws from any metrical theories available if they contribute to a better understanding of a given metrical phenomenon. Exercises and suggestions for further reading can be found in each chapter so that the book can serve as a textbook for the classroom or self-study. Possible answers to the exercises are provided in Appendix A.

I shall also take up problems of textual criticism here. Given the recent trend of textual conservatism, many scholars, particularly editors of Old English verse texts, tend to be somewhat hesitant about emending texts based on metrical evidence alone, since they do not regard the rules of metre as rigid and reliable enough to support textual emendation (cf. Duggan 1988).[2] Of course, we must always be cautious about emending any manuscript readings and 'we must not force what looks metrically attractive on to a passage the likely sense and obvious syntax of which are against

2 Fulk (1997) illustrates with scepticism the prevalence of textual conservatism in recent years. For conservative attitudes, see Hoops (1932), Gneuss (1973), Stanley (1984), Niles (1994), and most recently Kiernan (2004). Among the few liberals are Sisam (1946, 1953) and Lapidge (1991, 1993, 1994). While Stanley states that every scribe, 'sleepy and careless as he may have been at times, knew his living Old English better than the best modern editor of Old English verse' (1984: 257), Lapidge recommends that we should 'liberate ourselves from the premise that the work of sleepy and careless scribes should be venerated above our own judgement' (1993: 157). Niles takes a conservative stance not 'out of a blind respect for medieval scribes' but 'out of regard for the singers or speakers the traces of whose words may linger in scribal records' (1994: 453).

it.'[3] At the same time, if a half-line or line shows any metrical irregularities in the light of firm statistical evidence, it might be at least worth making a closer examination of the relevant half-line or line, which might reveal grammatical, semantic and/or palaeographical anomalies otherwise unnoticed. Knowledge of metre, I believe, never ceases to be relevant to students working in the field of Old English poetry.

A few words about metrical 'rules' or 'laws,' which I often refer to when I take up questions of textual criticism. In most cases, I use these terms to indicate statistically confirmed tendencies but not categorical rules. The laws are not prescriptive, either. When they preferred certain metrical forms according to the rules, the poets did not, I believe, make any deliberate choice of the 'right' pattern but intuitively felt which sounded metrically better.

A majority of the illustrative examples are taken from *Beowulf*, which has generally been regarded as the reference point for Old English metrical studies, but other verse texts are used as needed. For the convenience of beginners, most examples in Old English are provided with literal modern English translations with glosses also added in the first three introductory chapters.

3 Stanley (1992: 281).

Acknowledgments

The final draft of this book was prepared during a period of sabbatical leave from April 2008 through March 2009 when I was a visiting scholar at Harvard University. I would like to thank my host institution as well as the University of Tokyo for enabling me to pursue this book project.

A few paragraphs of chapter 4.1 were taken in revised form from my '*Beowulf* niokeru 3 onsetsu ika hangyo nitsuite' [Notes on Half-lines of Three or Fewer Syllables in *Beowulf*] in *Essays on* Beowulf *and Other Medieval English Literature in Memory of Kinshiro Oshitari*; portions of chapter 5 appeared in 'Agent-Nouns in *-end*: The Use of Alternative Plurals as Metrical Variants in Old English Poetry' in *Language and Beyond: A Festschrift for Hiroshi Yonekura on the Occasion of His 65th Birthday*, 'The Scarcity of Formations in *-ere* in Old English Poetry' in *Anglia*, and 'Metrical Constraints on Old English Compounds' in *Poetica*; and part of chapter 6.1.3 was published under the title 'The Weak Man in Old English Poetry' in *Journal of English and Germanic Philology*. I am grateful to the editors and publishers concerned for permission to reuse material.

In the process of writing the book, I have been fortunate to have the support and guidance of a number of colleagues and friends, and I especially wish to thank the following: Eric Stanley, without whose wisdom, scholarship, and insight the present book would be much the poorer; Rick Russom, who has been a mentor since I wrote my dissertation and as ever gave invariably constructive suggestions; Daniel Donoghue, who made my stay at Harvard productive through stimulating discussions on Old English metre.

I also owe a debt of gratitude to Paul Davenport and Brendan Wilson, both of whom read the draft very carefully and suggested numerous stylistic improvements. Many thanks go to Kiriko Sato, who thoroughly checked quotations and bibliographic details.

This book has benefited from suggestions made by two anonymous readers for the Press, to whom thanks are also due. The University of Toronto Press has been efficient, patient, and courteous, and I would like to thank Suzanne Rancourt, Barb Porter, Miriam Skey, and the series editor, Andy Orchard.

Last but not least, I am grateful to my parents for their moral support, and to my wife and daughter for their ever encouraging smiles.

OLD ENGLISH METRE: AN INTRODUCTION

1 Introduction

Overview

This chapter serves as a preliminary to the following chapters. I provide a sketch of two important features of Old English metre, alliteration and rhythm. We shall also see how these features relate to grammar and word-choice in the poetry and how this knowledge will lead to the better reading of extant poetic texts.

1.1 Alliteration

One of the most conspicuous features of Old English poetry is ALLITERATION, a repetition of the same sound at the beginning of two or more stressed words in a line (alliterating letters are in boldface type):[1]

```
 /        /                 /       /
fēasceaft funden.   Hē þæs frōfre gebād                    (Beo 7)
destitute   found   he for-that consolation experienced
[(he was) found destitute.   For that, he lived to see consolation]
```

As indicated by spacing, a (long) line is usually divided by a CAESURA or pause between the ON-VERSE (also known as the a-verse or the first half-line) and the OFF-VERSE (also known as the b-verse or the second

1 The *Beowulf* text used is Fulk, Bjork, and Niles (2008). Other verse instances to be given later are cited chiefly from Krapp-Dobbie (1931–53). For short titles of prose texts as well as verse texts, I follow Healey-Venezky (1980).

half-line).[2] Each verse or half-line usually contains two LIFTs or rhythmically stressed syllables, which can participate in alliteration. Lifts are marked with a stroke (/). In the line above, alliteration falls on two lifts of the on-verse and only on the first lift of the off-verse, but there are long lines in which only the first lift of each half-line alliterates. Alliterating lifts are marked 'A' and non-alliterating lifts marked 'X' and 'Y':

/ / / /
on flōdes ǣht feor gewītan (*Beo* 42)
in of-ocean possession far go
A X A Y
[(many treasures should) go far into the possession of the ocean]

Placement of alliteration is rule-governed. In *Beowulf* and other Old English poetry, for instance, DOUBLE ALLITERATION (i.e., the occurrence of two alliterating lifts in a half-line) is allowed in the on-verse but not in the off-verse. Thus, the following hypothetical lines with double alliteration in the off-verse would not be metrically acceptable in Old English. An asterisk indicates that an example is unmetrical or unattested:[3]

/ / / /
****m**ǣrne be **m**æste. Þǣr wæs **m**āððum **m**onig (cf. *Beo* 36)
famous by mast there was treasure many
A A A A
[the famous one by the mast. There was many a treasure]

/ / / /
***m**ǣrne þēoden. Þǣr wæs **m**āððum **m**onig
famous lord there was treasure many
A X A A
[the famous lord. There was many a treasure]

2 In manuscript, verse texts are written continuously without line or half-line divisions, like prose texts. Some manuscripts (e.g., the Junius MS) systematically mark the divisions with a certain punctuation.

3 This use of the asterisk differs from its use in historical linguistics where the asterisk denotes that the form is not recorded but is a probable reconstruction. The two uses, however, agree in showing that the form marked with the symbol is not attested.

The off-verse is subject to a further constraint: only the first lift can participate in alliteration; in fact, it must participate in alliteration. The following off-verses with alliteration only on the second lift would have sounded anomalous to an Old English audience:

/ / / /
*wæs se grimma gǣst hāten Grendel (cf. *Beo* 102)
was the fierce demon called Grendel
A A X A
[the fierce demon was called Grendel]

/ / / /
*on flōdes ǣht gewītan feor (cf. *Beo* 42 above)
in of-ocean possession go far
A X Y A

Although less strictly than in the off-verse, the alliterative pattern is also constrained in the on-verse, which rarely allows the second lift alone to take part in alliteration:

/ / / /
*on ǣht flōdes feor gewītan (cf. *Beo* 42 above)
in possession of-ocean far go
X A A Y

To sum up, the basic alliterative schemes in a long line of Old English poetry are represented as [AA: AY] and [AX: AY], where the colon indicates the caesura between the two half-lines.

EXERCISE: Alliterative Patterns

Observe the alliterative patterns in the following half-lines. Lifts are marked with a stroke (/). Which lines are metrically acceptable and which unacceptable? Provide an explanation for your judgment.

/ / / /
1) feorran ond nēan þā þū nū hafast
far and near that you now have
[(gifts) that you now have from far and near]

```
   /       /                 /    /
2) mildum wordum,      swā sceal man dōn
   generous with-words   as shall one   do
   [with generous words as one ought to do]

   /            /             /     /
3) wordum bewægned,    ond gold wunden
   with-words offered       and gold twisted
   [(invitation was) offered in words and twisted gold (was presented)]

   /         /               /   /
4) windige weallas.      Wyrd oft nereð
   windy    cliffs             fate    often saves
   [the windy cliffs.      Often fate saves (an undoomed man)]

                   /       /         /       /
5) Ðǣr wæs on hring-sele       hæleþa hleahtor
   there was in ring-hall            men's laughter
   [There was in the ring-hall laughter among men]
```

1.2 How Alliteration Affects Grammar and Word-choice

Knowledge of the alliterative patterns described above helps us to see why in the following off-verse the *Beowulf* poet used the 'noun-adjective' order, for which prose writers would have resorted to the reverse order. 'N' and 'ADJ' stand for 'noun' and 'adjective' respectively:

```
   /      /               /       /
**hæleð hīofende,      hlāford lēofne                        (Beo 3142)
                           N       ADJ
men    lamenting       lord      beloved
[the lamenting men (laid down) the beloved lord]
```

The 'normal' word order (i.e., adjective-noun) would result in an unmetrical off-verse with alliteration on the second lift rather than the first:

```
    /      /               /        /
*hæleð hīofende,      lēofne hlāford
                        ADJ     N
 men    lamenting       beloved lord
```

Note that the adjective *lēof* precedes the noun in the off-verse below, where alliteration falls on /l/:

/ / / /
ālēdon þā lēofne þēoden (*Beo* 34)
laid then beloved king
[then (they) laid down the beloved king]

An understanding of alliteration also provides an explanation for the abundance of compounds in Old English poetry, another significant feature of traditional diction. Consider the following line in *Beowulf*:

/ / / /
gūðbilla nān, grētan nolde (*Beo* 803)
of-battle-swords none touch not-would
[none of the battle-swords would touch (the foe)]

It is true that in *gūð-bill* 'battle-sword,' *gūð* adds a poetical glory to the simple word. The first compound element, however, has a semantically redundant relation to the second. Swords generally exist for the sake of battle. The poet uses this pleonastic compound instead of the simple word *bill* because it gives alliteration on the sound *g* between *gūðbilla* and *grētan*. Similarly, the poet might substitute *hilde-* for *gūð-* to provide alliteration on *h*, as in the following line:

/ / / /
hildebille; **h**eaþoræ̅s fornam (*Beo* 557)
with-battle-sword battle-storm took-away
[with the battle-sword; the force of battle carried off (the sea-beast)]

1.3 Rhythm

The subtleties of Old English metre reside not only in patterns of alliteration but also in rules of syllable count and stress. Each half-line normally contains two lifts or rhythmically stressed syllables whereas the number of unstressed syllables may vary. Thus, unlike most post-Conquest poetry, Old English verse texts do not strictly regulate the number of syllables either in a half-line or in a line: some half-lines consist of four syllables (i.e., two rhythmically stressed syllables and two unstressed syllables) and others of nine or even more (i.e., two rhythmically stressed syllables and seven or more unstressed syllables), excluding so-called hypermetric verses. 'a' and 'b' after a line number (e.g., 66a, 1298b) represent the a-verse (i.e., the on-verse) and the b-verse (i.e., the off-verse), respectively:

/ /
georne hȳrdon (*Beo* 66a)
willingly heard
[(they) willingly obeyed (him)]

/ /
þone ðe hēo on ræste ābrēat (*Beo* 1298b)
whom she on rest killed
[whom she killed on the resting-place]

Although the number of syllables might vary in a half-line, there is one fundamental requirement: each half-line must contain at least four syllables, as we shall see in more detail in 4.1. This requirement interacts with poetic grammar and word-choice.

1.4 How Rhythm Affects Grammar and Word-choice

In Old English, both uninflected and inflected infinitives occur after *tō*. The inflected ending in *–anne* is in origin the dative case of a verbal noun:

Mǣl is mē tō *fēran* (*Beo* 316a)
time is for-me to go
[It is time for me to go]

tō *healdanne* (*Beo* 1731a)
to hold
[to hold]

The use of inflected *healdanne* is due to metrical requirements.[4] The uninflected *healdan* would make 1731a too short a verse, with only three syllables:

*tō healdan

4 In *Beowulf*, on the other hand, the inflected (manuscript) form has sometimes been changed to the uninflected form for the sake of metre. See Bliss (1967: § 44) and Fulk, Bjork, and Niles (2008: 328–9, § 21).

Needless to say, good poets like the *Beowulf* poet could recast the (half-) line entirely to avoid the problem altogether rather than being forced to choose between metrical variants. Yet the availability of two semantically and grammatically equivalent forms provides a convenient option in verse-making.

EXERCISE: The Four-syllable Principle and Word-choice

The *Beowulf* poet sometimes satisfies the 'four syllable per half-line' requirement by choosing between two morphological variants. In the epic, for instance, there appear eleven instances of *gēn* 'still' while the alternative form with the suffix *–a* (derived from the adverb *ā* 'ever') is attested twice. Consider the following half-line where one of the two instances of *gēna* occurs:

fremmað gēna (*Beo* 2800b)
attend to still
[now attend to (the people's need)]

Why do you think the poet used the rarer form *gēna* instead of ordinary *gēn*?

1.5 Textual Criticism

Old English metre can be of great help in textual criticism. Corruptions are often found in Old English manuscripts due to scribal error or physical damage in the course of transmission. When corruptions are not obvious at first glance, knowledge of Old English metre can help us to identify them and guide us toward better readings. Consider the following line as it appears in the *Beowulf* manuscript:

þæt hē for handgripe mīnum scolde (*Beo* 965)
that he for hand-grip my should
[so that he should (lie struggling for life) because of my hand-grip]

This is part of a speech made by Beowulf after defeating Grendel: the hero has tried to kill the monster by his handgrip (*handgripe*) but Grendel has vanished, leaving his arm behind. Although it does not exhibit any semantic or grammatical problem, the line lacks alliteration. As the word *mund* is synonymous with *hand*, we may suspect that the original reading was *mundgripe*:

þæt hē for ***mu***ndgripe **mī**num scolde

Most editors of *Beowulf* today adopt this emendation on the assumption that *handgripe* was introduced by the scribe, who would have been more familiar with *hand* than with archaic *mund*.[5]

Let us now turn to another half-line from *Beowulf* as it appears in the manuscript:

brād **b**rūnecg (*Beo* 1546a)
broad bright-edged
[broad (and) bright-edged]

The two adjectives in juxtaposition refer to the dagger drawn by Grendel's mother. Syntactically, this verse is legitimate, since Old English poetry allows so-called asyndetic constructions where two elements are conjoined without a conjunction. With only three syllables, however, the verse is too short. To amend the metrical difficulty, most editors insert the conjunction *ond* between the two adjectives:

brād [ond] **b**rūnecg

This conjecture has been widely supported, perhaps in part because the conjunction appears in a parallel half-line from the *Battle of Maldon* (*brād and brūneccg* 163a).[6]

In the following chapters, we explore the interesting realm of Old English metre with reference to alliteration, rhythm, how these features affect the word-formation/word-choice and grammar of poetry, and how knowledge of Old English metre can lead to better understanding of the poetic

5 Kiernan, however, admits non-alliterating lines as 'intelligent variation rather than scribal corruption' (1996: 185). Niles (1994) also regards the manuscript reading *handgripe* as preferable since it indicates 'a rough and ready quality in the poet's artistry that reveals itself in an indifference to alliterative norms even when these norms could easily be satisfied' (1994: 457–8).

6 For the editorial readings of *Beo* 1546a, see the *apparatus criticus* of Fulk, Bjork, and Niles (2008: 53). Niles follows the manuscript, stating that '[t]he rule that a verse requires a minimum of four syllables is a modern one, and there is no way to test for a consciousness of it on the part of Anglo-Saxon poets' (1994: 459).

texts. Let us start with alliteration, the most noticeable feature of Old English poetry.

References and Suggestions for Further Reading

For readings on alliteration and rhythm in Old English poetry and their relevance to grammar and word-choice, see 'References and Suggestions for Further Reading' in chapters 2 through 6. Gade and Fulk (2000) provide a more detailed bibliography of Old English and Germanic alliterative metre. See also the yearly updates in relevant sections of 'Old English Bibliography' and 'The Year's Work in Old English Studies' in the *Old English Newsletter*.

The importance of metre for textual studies is emphasized by Fulk (1997) and Bredehoft (2005b). Irving also recommends that when they encounter metrical irregularities, editors should 'suggest a remedy where possible or supply an obvious word' rather than '[s]crapping or ignoring the formal system of verse' (1998: 17). For scepticism about the use of metrical evidence for emendation, see Duggan (1988) and Niles (1994) among others.

2 Alliteration

Overview

Alliteration is one of the most significant traits of Old English poetry. The alliterating words usually have the same initial sound, as in *fēasceaft funden. / Hē þæs frōfre gebād* (*Beo* 7) discussed at the beginning of the preceding chapter. This is, however, not the whole story. Although they share the same initial consonant, *stān* 'stone' and *sand* 'sand' do not form an alliterating pair in Old English verse. On the other hand, *æþelingas* 'nobles' and *ellen* 'courage,' which have different initial vowels, are regarded as an alliterating pair. What exactly makes two sounds suitable for alliteration? As we saw in chapter 1, the placement of alliteration is highly regulated. Why did Old English poets avoid such a line as **wæs se grimma gǣst / hāten Grendel*, where the off-verse (following the slash) has alliteration only on the second lift? Does one part of speech take precedence in alliteration over another part of speech? And while alliteration clearly plays the leading part, what position does end-rhyme hold in the Old English poetic corpus? Let us begin by examining consonantal and vocalic alliteration.

2.1 Consonantal and Vocalic Alliteration

In Old English poetry, as we have already seen, the two half-lines are linked by alliteration, a repetition of the initial sound (of a stressed syllable) in two or more words:

sē ðe gryresīðas gegān dorste (*Beo* 1462)
who horror-expeditions go dared
[who dared to go on dreadful expeditions]

For consonantal alliteration, repetition of a single consonant usually suffices. In the instance above, *gryresīðas* and *-gān* alliterate on /g/. Since they are normally unstressed, prefixes like *ge-* do not take part in alliteration.

The initial consonant clusters *sp-* and *st-* generally alliterate with exactly the same consonant groups respectively. The same is true of *sc-*, which is pronounced /ʃ/ as in the initial sound of Present-day English *show*:

spēd wrecan **sp**el gerāde (*Beo* 873)
and in success recite story apt
[and (he began to) successfully tell an apt story]

ond on **sp**ēd wrecan **sp**el gerāde

Strǣt wæs **st**ānfāh, **st**īg wīsode (*Beo* 320)
street was stone-adorned path led
[The road was paved with stone, a path guided (the men)]

Scyldes eafera **Sc**edelandum in (*Beo* 19)
Scyld's son Danish-lands in
[the son of Scyld (was renowned) in the Danish lands]

★ **Alliteration between *sc-/sp-/st-* and *s-***

In the *Paris Psalter*, which is known to show quite a few metrical irregularities, the combination *sc-* alliterates with the single consonant *s-* as well as *sc-*, although *sp-* and *st-* regularly alliterate with the same clusters:

sceame **sc**eandlīce þe þīnes **s**īðes hēr (*PPs* 68.7.2)
shame shamefully who of-your-journey here
[(No one shall have) disgrace shamefully who (waits for) your journey here]

Exceptional alliteration between *sc-* and *s-* is otherwise attested perhaps three times in the Old English poetic corpus, in the *Lord's Prayer II* (84), the *Death of Alfred* (19), and the *Judgment Day II* (169), the three poems all being late. The last two instances are, however, doubtful. In Ælfric's rhythmical prose, *s-* alliterates with *sp-/st-* as well as *sc-*. See 7.3 below.

In Old English, there are two varieties of *g*, one velar (as in the initial *g* of Present-day English *gas*) and the other palatalized (as in the initial *y* of Present-day English *yes*). At the beginning of a word, palatal *g* occurs before front vowels (e.g., /i, e, y/) and diphthongs beginning with front vowels. For the reader's convenience, this variety of *g* is marked with a dot above it, thus ġ, when alliteration matters. In so-called classical poems like

Beowulf, these two sounds (originally identical) are usually treated as equivalent for purposes of alliteration. In the line below, velar *g* in *God* alliterates with the palatalized counterpart in *geong* and *geardum*:

ġeong in ġeardum, þone God sende (*Beo* 13)
young in dwellings whom God sent
[a young (son was born) in the court, whom God had sent]

In the *Battle of Maldon*, which was obviously composed after the year of the battle (i.e., AD 991), a distinction is made between the two different *g*'s, probably because the late poet no longer adhered to the earlier metrical practice.[1] Thus, the *Maldon* poet allows matching between velar *g*'s or between palatalized *g*'s, but not between different *g*'s (see 7.1). In the following half-lines from *Maldon*, the velar *g*'s alliterate with each other in the first instance whereas in the second instance the palatalized *g*'s form an alliterating pair:

gār tō gūþe. Hē hæfde gōd geþanc (*Mald* 13)
spear to battle he had good thought
[(he carried) his spear to the battle. He had a firm mind]

ġearo and ġeornful, ġylpwordum spræc (*Mald* 274)
ready and eager with-boasting-words spoke
[(he stood) ready and eager, spoke with vaunting words]

Just as in the case of the two different *g*'s, alliteration occurs between the two varieties of word-initial *c*-, i.e., velar *c* (as in the initial *k* of Present-day English *king*) and palatal *c* (as in the initial *ch* of Present-day English *chill*; marked with a dot above). (Palatal *c* occurs in the same environment as palatal *g*.) Interestingly, the *Maldon* poet, who avoided alliterating between the different *g*'s, allowed alliteration between the different *c*'s, although alliteration on the letter 'c' occurs only once:

cāfne mid his cynne, þæt wæs Ċēolan sunu (*Mald* 76)[2]
valiant amid his family that was Ceola's son
[(he was) valiant amid his family, he was a son of Ceola]

---

1 According to Bliss (1962: § 14), 'the two sounds [velar and palatal g] alliterate freely together until about the year 1000.'

2 In *cynne*, *c* remained unpalatalized /k/ because *y* resulted from *i*-umlaut (cf. Gmc **kunjam*).

The initial consonant *h-* can be treated as silent. In *Juliana*, the proper name *Heliseus* always alliterates with words that begin with a vowel:

H**e**liseus **ē**hstrēam sōhte (*Jul* 673)
Eleusius sea sought
[Eleusius went to sea]

But a word with initial *h-* could be ambivalent. In *Beowulf*, the adverb *hraðe* 'quickly' alliterates with *(ge)rymed* and *rica* in line 1975 whereas the same word also alliterates on /h/ in lines like 1576:

H**r**aðe wæs ge**r**ȳmed, swā se **r**īca bebēad (*Beo* 1975)
quickly was cleared as the powerful-one commanded
[(The floor) was quickly cleared, as the powerful one commanded]

hilderince, ac hē **h**raþe wolde (*Beo* 1576)
to-battle-warrior but he quickly wished
[(The sword was not useless) to the warrior but he quickly wanted (to repay)]

In the *Beowulf* manuscript, the name of Hrothgar's courtier appears as *Hunferð* with initial *h-* (cf. also ll. 530, 1165, 1488):

H**u**nferð maþelode, **E**cglāfes bearn (*Beo* 499)
Unferth spoke Ecglaf's son
[Unferth, Ecglaf's son, spoke]

Since this name always alliterates with a vowel, it is likely that *Unferð* was the form intended by the poet—thus 'h' in *Hunferð* has often been omitted in editions of *Beowulf*. The scribal addition of inorganic *h-* would be due to analogical influence of Germanic names in *Hun-*, such as *Hūnlāfing* (cf. *Beo* 1143), *Hūnlāf*, and the like.[3]

In Old English poetry, alliteration may occur between initial vowels:

egsode **eo**rlas, syððan **ǣ**rest wearð (*Beo* 6)
terrified men after first became
[(he) terrified men, after (he) was first (found destitute)]

3 In *Beowulf*, *ondlean* 'requital' and *ondslyht* 'counterblow,' both of which alliterate with vowels, are always spelled with initial *h-* in the manuscript (cf. ll. 1541, 2094, 2929, 2972).

ǣnne ofer ȳðe **u**mborwesende (*Beo* 46)
alone over waves being-a-child
[(they sent him forth) alone across the waves being still a child]

As we see from the instances above, vocalic alliteration can take place between different vowels/diphthongs, and in fact alliteration of the same vowels tends to be avoided. The absence of identical vocalic alliteration might suggest that what really alliterates in vocalic alliteration is not the vowels but an underlying prevocalic 'glottal stop' /ʔ/—the sound that is heard in Present-day English between adjacent vowels as in *co-operate*.

EXERCISE: Consonantal and Vocalic Alliteration

Identify which sounds alliterate in the following lines from *Beowulf*:

1) geongum gārwigan gēoce gefremman (*Beo* 2674)
young spear-warrior help perform
[(the mail-coat could not) provide the young spear-warrior with any help]

2) cūþe næssas; ċēol up geþrang (*Beo* 1912)
well-known headlands ship up pressed
[the well-known headlands; the ship pressed forward]

3) stōd on stapole, geseah stēapne hrōf (*Beo* 926)
stood on steps saw steep roof
[(he) stood on the steps, saw the lofty roof]

4) idese tō efnanne, þēah ðe hīo ǣnlicu sȳ (*Beo* 1941)
woman to perform though she peerless be
[for a woman to perform, even though she may be peerless in beauty]

5) Ārīs, rīces weard, uton hraþe fēran (*Beo* 1390)
arise of-kingdom guardian let-us quickly go
[Stand up, guardian of the kingdom, let us go quickly]

2.2 Alliterative Patterns in the Line and Half-line

2.2.1 Anomalous Alliteration

As we saw in 1.1, there is a rather strict constraint on the distribution of the alliterating syllables in a line: the off-verse allows only the first lift to take part in alliteration. Hence breaches of this constraint are symptoms of textual corruption. In the *Beowulf* manuscript, there are four apparent instances of double alliteration in the off-verse:

Đā wæs **h**eal **h**roden (*Beo* 1151b)
then was hall covered
[Then the hall was covered]

hilde ge**h**nǣgdon (*Beo* 2916b)
in-battle humbled
[(they) humbled (him) in battle]

in ēowrum **g**ūð**g**eatawum (*Beo* 395b)
in your war-equipments
[in your war-equipments]

þæt ic mid **s**weorde of**s**lōh (*Beo* 574b)
that I with sword slew
[that I slew (sea-monsters) with a sword]

In the first two instances, as inorganic *h* is sometimes added to the beginning of a word in the epic (cf. *Hunferð* discussed above in 2.1 and *hnægde* [=*nǣgde* 'addressed'] 1318), *hroden* and *(ge)hnǣgdon* should be emended to *roden* 'reddened' and *genǣgdon* 'attacked' respectively. In the third instance, it has been suggested that the second element of *gūð-geatawum* could be slightly altered to *ge-tāwum* 'apparatus' where the unstressed prefix *ge-* would not alliterate. These emendations, which are palaeographically as well as metrically plausible, have been accepted in most recent editions of *Beowulf*.

EXERCISE: To Emend or Not to Emend

In the last instance above (*Beo* 574b) where double alliteration occurs in the off-verse, consult the editions of *Beowulf* available to you and check whether the editors follow the manuscript reading or provide an emendation. Do you support an emendation? If not, give reasons.

2.2.2 *Crossed and Transverse Alliteration*

Besides the regular alliterative patterns (i.e., [AA: AX], [AX: AY], or rarely [XA: AY]), there appear sporadic instances of ornate alliterative patterns. The following line shows what is called CROSSED ALLITERATION, in which all four lifts in a line participate in alliteration in the pattern [AB: AB]. Alliteration between the second and fourth lift should be regarded as ornamental and distinguished from the systematic alliteration between the first and third lift:

snottra **f**engel, nū ic eom **s**īðes **f**ūs (*Beo* 1475)
wise king now I am of-journey ready
A B A B
[(Be mindful,) wise king, now I am ready for the venture]

There occurs another type of ornate alliteration, [AB: BA], named TRANSVERSE ALLITERATION, though it is less frequent than the pattern [AB: AB]:[4]

brūnfāgne **h**elm, **h**ringde **b**yrnan (*Beo* 2615)
shining helmet ringed corslet
A B B A
[the shining helmet, the corslet made of ring-mail]

4 The usage of the terms 'crossed alliteration' (sometimes 'cross alliteration') and 'transverse alliteration' varies among scholars; Lehmann and Tabusa (1958) and Le Page (1959) use 'crossed alliteration' for both types; Cassidy and Ringler (1971) employs 'transverse alliteration' as an umbrella term; Baker (2007) calls [AB: AB] 'transverse alliteration' and [AB: BA] 'crossed alliteration.'

A more intricate use of alliteration (sometimes called 'linked alliteration') can be observed in *Elene*, a verse rendering of the legend of the finding of the Cross by St Helena:[5]

Here wīcode,
eorlas ymb æðeling, ēgstrēame nēah
on nēaweste nihtlangne fyrst,
þæs þe hīe fēonda gefær fyrmest gesǣgon.
Þā wearð on slǣpe sylfum ætȳwed
þām cāsere, þǣr hē on corðre swæf,
sigerōfum gesegen swefnes wōma.
Þūhte him wlitescȳne on weres hāde
hwīt ond hīwbeorht hæleða nāthwylc
geȳwed ǣnlīcra þonne hē ǣr oððe sīð
gesēge under swegle (*El* 65b–75a)

[The army encamped—the warriors (were) around the prince—near the river-stream in their neighbourhood for the night period, after they had first seen the expedition of their enemies. Then (there) was revealed in sleep to the emperor himself, as he slept among his company, a vision of a dream (was) seen by the triumphant man. (It) seemed to him a beautiful (being) in human form, white and radiant, some man appeared more beautiful than he had seen early or late under the sky.]

Note that in the passage above the initial sound of the second lift in the off-verse often anticipates the alliteration in the following line: the last word *nēah* in line 66 is, for instance, alliteratively linked with *nēaweste* and *nihtlangne* in the next line. The sounds in linked alliteration are underlined.

2.2.3 Explaining Alliterative Patterns

Why does only the first lift of the off-verse take part in alliteration but not both or only the second lift? And why is it rare to find on-verses in which only the second lift takes part in alliteration if we disregard the questionable type [XA: AY] where weakly stressed elements comprise the first lift in the on-verse? Consider first the following half-line that consists exclu-

5 Creed (1993) discusses the use of linked alliteration ('enjambed alliteration' in his term) in *Beowulf*.

sively of a compound. For the reader's convenience, a hyphen is inserted between compound elements:

/ /
hilde-lēoman (*Beo* 1143b, 2583a)
[battle-gleamer]

/ /
mere-līðende (*Beo* 255a)
[sea-farers]

Half-lines of this sort, which often occur in Old English poetry, would suggest that the metrical structure of a half-line 'mimics' the stress pattern of a compound: just as the stress on the first element (i.e., *hilde-*, *mere-*) is stronger than that on the second element (i.e., *-lēoman, -līðende*), so the first lift in a half-line receives stronger rhythmic stress than the second lift.

The metrical structure of a long line also reflects the compound stress pattern in that the on-verse is metrically more prominent than the off-verse. Consequently, double alliteration can occur in the on-verse but is not allowed in the off-verse. The metrical structure of a line and a half-line is represented in the following tree diagram:[6]

Metrical Tree Structure of a Line and a Half-line (S and W stand for 'metrically strong' and 'metrically weak' respectively.)

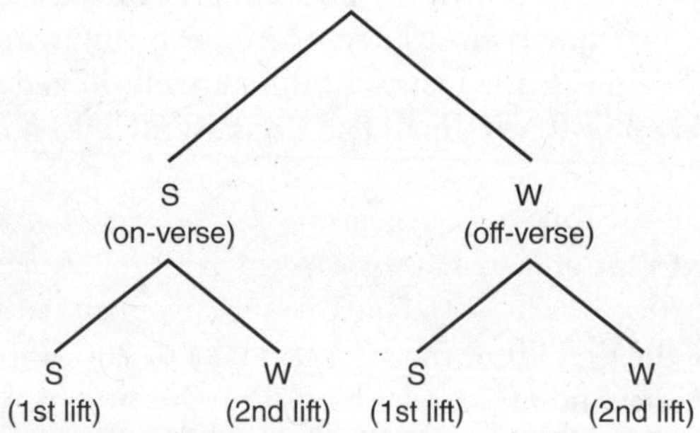

6 See Russom (1987: 71). Donoghue (1990: 71), however, finds Russom's tree-based analysis problematic because the first lift of the off-verse, which has often been regarded as metrically most prominent, is governed by a weak node. From the viewpoint of verse composition, however, it would be more natural that the first lift of the on-verse linearly preceding that of the off-verse be a determining factor in alliteration. See Fujiwara (1990: 231).

This metrical structure correctly predicts the distribution of alliteration in a line and a half-line: as the second lift of the off-verse governed by two W's is the weakest metrical constituent, it should not alliterate; on the other hand, the first lifts of both half-lines, which are the stronger metrical constituents in their respective half-lines, always take part in alliteration.

2.3 The Alliterative Rule of Precedence

Let us take another look at the pattern of alliteration with reference to the parts of speech of alliterating words:

ellen fremedon (*Beo* 3b)
courage performed
N FV
[(they) performed courageous deeds]

Geseah hē in recede (*Beo* 728a)
saw he in hall
FV N
[He saw (many warriors) in the hall]

In these half-lines consisting of a noun (N) and a finite verb (FV), regardless of the order of the two elements, alliteration falls on the former (i.e., *ellen* 'courage' and *recede* 'hall') but not on the latter (i.e., *fremedon* 'performed,' *geseah* 'saw'). In Old English poetry, a nominal (including an adjective, a participle, and an infinitive as well as a noun) normally takes precedence in alliteration over a finite verb. This priority of a nominal over a finite verb is known as the **ALLITERATIVE RULE OF PRECEDENCE**.

★★ Breaches of the Rule of Precedence

The Alliterative Rule of Precedence is violated in the following off-verse from *Beowulf* where the finite verb precedes the two nouns in alliteration:

seah on enta geweorc (*Beo* 2717b)
saw on giants' work
FV N N
[(he) looked at the work of giants]

To remedy this anomaly, Donoghue (1987b: 38) has suggested that the sequence *seah on* be regarded as a scribal corruption of the infinitive *sēon*, which depends on the main verb *gīong* 'went' in verse 2715a. Note that infinitives are metrically as important as nouns. Although it is rather rare for the verb to have priority in alliteration over the noun in *Beowulf*, breaches of the Alliterative Rule of Precedence do occur in the epic (cf. 1128b, 1137b, 1327b, 1441b, 1537a, 1548b, 1872b, 2544b, 2863b, 2980b) and more frequently in the other verse texts (cf. *Sat* 631b; *Mald* 7a, 127b, 128b, 240b, 242b). The violations are especially noticeable in the off-verse where the demand for alliteration on the first lift is pressing. Thus, the reinterpretation of *seah on* as an infinitive might not be necessary.

If an on-verse contains two nominals, say a noun and an adjective, alliteration falls on both words or on the word at the left, but not on the word at the right alone:

swǣse ge**s**īþas (*Beo* 29a)
own retainers
[(his) own retainers]

lange hwīle (*Beo* 16a)
long while
[for a long while]

In verse 16a, although syntactically the noun *hwīle* 'while' serves as the head of the noun phrase, the adjective *lange* 'long' at the left alliterates in precedence to the noun. This tendency is called **LEFT DOMINANCE**, which is considered to be a manifestation of the compound stress pattern (SW) at the half-line level (cf. 2.2.3 above).[7] Interestingly, breaches of this principle occur in a late poem:

Ælfere and **M**accus (*Mald* 80a)

Although the two proper nouns are of equal metrical prominence, it is only the right element (i.e., *Maccus*) that alliterates.

7 Pope-Fulk (2001) use the term 'Rule of Precedence' for our Left Dominance.

EXERCISE: Breaches of the Alliterative Rules

As mentioned above, the *Battle of Maldon* often shows irregularities in alliteration. Consider the following half-lines from this late poem and explain how the use of alliteration deviates from the norm. Alliterating letters are in bold type.

1) hē **l**ēt him þā of handon (*Mald* 7a)
he let him then off hands
[he then let (his hawk fly) off his hands]

2) hwæt þis folc **s**egeð (*Mald* 45b)
what this people says
[what this nation says]

3) sē wæs hāten **W**ulfstān (*Mald* 75b)
he was called Wulfstan
[he was called Wulfstan]

4) scyldburh tō**b**rocen (*Mald* 242a)
shield-wall broken
[the shield-wall (was) broken]

5) **Þ**urstānes **s**unu (*Mald* 298a)
Thurstan's son
[the son of Thurstan]

Although alliteration normally falls on nouns, adjectives, and verbs, weak forms like pronouns and prepositions occasionally receive rhythmic stress and participate in alliteration:

ge**h**ēdde under **h**eofenum þonne **h**ē sylfa (*Beo* 505)
might-care-for under heavens than he himself
[(any other man) might care for (more glories) under the heavens than he himself]

on **þ**ǣm dæge **þ**ysses līfes (*Beo* 197)
on that day this of-life
[at that time of this life]

folces gefylled beforan þissum (*Brun* 67)
of-people killed before this
[(no greater number) of people (has been) killed before this]

In the first instance, perhaps for the sake of emphasis, the personal pronoun forms the first lift of the off-verse so as to alliterate. In the second instance, which seems to be formulaic (cf. *Beo* 790, 806), alliteration on the demonstratives *þæm* and *þysses* might indicate rhetorical contrast between the distant past and the contemporary Anglo-Saxon period. In the verse from the *Battle of Brunanburh*, the stem syllable of the preposition *beforan* 'before' alliterates on /f/, bringing into focus the unprecedented cost in casualties.

2.4 Rhyme

In Old English and other Germanic languages, primary stress normally falls on the initial syllable of a word (except for words with certain prefixes). It naturally follows that end-rhyme plays a restricted role in Old English verse, usually serving as an optional embellishment to the verse-organizing alliteration. There appear occasional rhyming pairs such as ***frōd** ond **gōd*** 'wise and good' (*Beo* 279), ***sǣl** ond **mǣl*** 'proper time and occasion' (*Beo* 1008), ***wordum** ond **bordum*** 'with words and shields' (*El* 24) and even a rhyming trio like ***flōd blōd gewōd*** 'blood pervaded the flood' (*Ex* 463). In the following verse from *Beowulf*, rhyme is found between the verse-final words in a line. Here rhyme as well as alliteration links the on-verse to the off-verse:

fylle gef**ǣgon**; fægere geþ**ǣgon** (*Beo* 1014)
in-feasting rejoiced courteously drank
[(they) rejoiced in feasting; (their kinsmen) courteously drank]

Such verse-final rhyme more often occurs in late poems like the *Battle of Maldon* (cf. also *Mald* 42, 282, 309):

ǣfre embe st**unde** hē sealde sume w**unde** (*Mald* 271)
ever about time he gave some wound
[repeatedly he inflicted some wound]

Here rhyme actually takes the place of alliteration: since the *Maldon* poet otherwise alliterates the cluster *st* with itself (not with *s*), *stunde* is less likely to alliterate with *sume* than to rhyme with *wunde*. As we shall see in 7.3, another late poem known as the *Death of Alfred* depends more heavily on rhyme, relegating alliteration to the background.

Although extended use of rhyme can be found in the epilogue to *Elene* (cf. ll. 1236–50), the *Riming Poem* in the Exeter Book, as the editorial title suggests, shows the most regular use of verse-final rhyme along with alliteration in the Old English poetic corpus. In this verse text, while it usually links the on-verse and the off-verse, rhyme sometimes extends much further. In the following passage, eight half-lines rhyme with each other in succession:

Scrifen scr**ād** gl**ād** þurh gesc**ād** in br**ād**,
wæs on lagustrēame l**ād**, þǣr mē leoþu ne bigl**ād**.
Hæfde ic hēanne h**ād**, ne wæs mē in healle g**ād**,
þæt þǣr rōf weord r**ād**. Oft þǣr rinc geb**ād** (*Rim* 13–16)

[The appointed ship sailed widely through a channel, the course was on the sea where the ship did not desert me. I had high rank, (there) was no lack for me in a hall where the brave company of men rode. Often a man experienced there ...]

References and Suggestions for Further Reading

Lehmann and Tabusa (1958) and most recently Hazome (2005) provide convenient alliterative concordances to *Beowulf* where alliterating words are alphabetically ordered with relevant lines cited.

For the treatment of the initial cluster *sc*-, *sp*-, and *st*- in Old English poetry, see Yamanouchi (1986), who examines alliteration on *sc*- in the *Paris Psalter*.

In the lines showing alliterative irregularities, while a majority of scholars and editors attempt to provide emendations, a few scholars (cf. Niles 1994; Kiernan 2004) accept the anomalies, following the manuscript readings.

Russom (1987), following Kuryłowizc (1970), provides an elegant account of possible alliterative patterns in a line/half-line in terms of 'metrical compounding.' Suzuki (1996a) also considers the metrical pattern of left dominance to be a reflection of Old English word-stress patterns.

Orchard (1995) demonstrates subtle and sophisticated techniques of 'ornamental alliteration.' Le Page (1959) provides instances of transverse (what he calls 'crossed') alliteration in *Beowulf* and *Elene* although the list includes some doubtful cases where he assumes weakly stressed words take part in alliteration (e.g., *Beo* 355, 535, 813, 1721, etc.).

The Alliterative Rule of Precedence and Left Dominance are credited to Rieger (1876: 24–5) and Sievers (1893: §23.2). Breaches of these rules have been examined by Stanley (1975), Lucas (1987), and Fujiwara (1990).

Some other interesting aspects of alliteration not dealt with in this chapter are discussed by Cronan, who examines synonymous simplexes with respect to alliterative frequencies, and by Minkova, who surveys the English alliterative tradition from Old English to late Middle English, with discussion of the peculiarities of initial *sc-/sk-*, *sp-*, *st-* (see Cronan 1986; Minkova 2003).

For the use of rhyme in Old English poetry, Macrae-Gibson (1987: 21–5) and Stanley (1988: 19–38, 53–4) are useful. Sievers (1893: §§ 99–102) also lists possible instances of rhyme in Old English poetry. By comparing rhyme in Old English and Old Saxon, Bredehoft (2005c) argues that rhyme within the half-line must have been part of traditional verse-craft rather than embellishment.

3 Rhythm: The Basics

Overview

In Old English poetry, as we saw in chapter 1, each line is made up of two parts, the on-verse and the off-verse. Each half-line usually contains two primary rhythmic stresses although the number of unstressed syllables in a half-line varies. A word's part of speech helps us to determine whether it bears rhythmic stress. The distribution of rhythmically stressed and unstressed syllables in a half-line is not random but highly regulated to yield the five basic types of verse rhythm. We also look at lengthened modifications of the basic types (known as hypermetric verses).

3.1 Stress-words, Particles, and Proclitics

The first step toward scanning a half-line (analysing its rhythmic pattern) is to determine which words bear rhythmic stress. Of course alliteration is a great help: unless it is accidental or ornamental, alliteration indicates primary rhythmic stress. But as only one alliterating word appears in the off-verse and single alliteration occurs also in the on-verse, it is often necessary to assign rhythmic stress to a word without alliterative guidance. In Old English poetry, we can to a certain extent predict which word bears rhythmic stress with reference to its category or part of speech.

Words in Old English poetry can be classified into three categories with three degrees of rhythmic stress: **STRESS-WORDS**, **PARTICLES**, and **PROCLITICS.**[1] Stress-words are always stressed. They include nouns,

1 The classification into 'stress-words,' 'particles,' and 'proclitics' is roughly based on that made by Kuhn (1933).

adjectives, non-finite verbs (i.e., infinitives and participles), many adverbs, and some 'heavy' pronouns (e.g., *gehwylc* 'each,' *gehwæþer* 'each (of two)'). Proclitics, which appear immediately before a stress-word so as to depend on it, do not normally receive rhythmic stress; they comprise prepositions, demonstratives, possessives, copulative conjunctions (e.g., *ne*, *ond*), and prefixes. Finally, particles lie midway between the other two categories: although not subordinated to any element, they do not have a fully semantic force and hence usually fail to receive stress. Particles include finite verbs, demonstrative adverbs, personal pronouns, demonstrative pronouns, and some conjunctions.

Particles and proclitics can bear rhythmic stress under certain conditions. In verse, particles are normally placed together at the beginning of the clause, either before or after the first stress-word while proclitics stand immediately before the stress-word they depend on. If displaced from these normal positions, particles and proclitics receive rhythmic stress. Compare the following two excerpts from *Beowulf*:

/ / /
þæs wǣron mid **Ē**otenum ecge cūðe (*Beo* 1145)
of-it were among the Jutes edges known
[The edges of it (=the sword) were known among the Jutes]

sǣlāca gefeah
of-lake-booties rejoiced

/ / / /
mægenbyrþenne þāra þe hē him **m**id hæfde (*Beo* 1624b–5)
with-might-load of-those-which he him with had
[(he) was happy with his lake-booties, the mighty-burden of those which he had with him]

In the first instance, the root syllables of each stress-word (*Ēotenum* 'the Jutes,' *ecge* 'edges,' *cūðe* 'known') are rhythmically stressed whereas particles (*þæs* 'of it,' *wǣron* 'were') and a proclitic (*mid* 'among') are placed in their normal positions without bearing stress. Note also that in the on-verse the first rhythmic stress is suppressed. In the second passage, on the other hand, the preposition *mid* bears rhythmic stress and alliterates because it is postposed after the pronoun (*him*) it depends on. In the relative clause introduced by *þāra þe*, the finite verb (*hæfde* 'had') also acquires rhythmic stress since it is separated from the other particles (*þāra þe*, *hē*, *him*) at the beginning of the clause.

Verbal prefixes like *ā-*, *be-*, *for-*, and *ge-* are proclitics closely bound to a stem and do not bear stress. The negative prefix *un-* may occasionally receive rhythmic stress, however:

/ / / /
sē þe un**m**urnlīce **m**ādmas dǣleþ (*Beo* 1756)
who ungrudgingly treasures distributes
[(another) who ungrudgingly distributes treasures]

/ / / /
ylda bearnum, **u**ndyrne cūð (*Beo* 150)
men's to-sons plainly known
[(it became) plainly known to the sons of men]

In line 1756, *un-* fails to receive rhythmic stress and the line alliterates with /m/ on *-murnlīce* and *mādmas.* In line 150, however, the prefix is stressed, taking part in vocalic alliteration with *ylda*.

The metrical status of *un-* is ambiguous in ***gold unrīme / grimme gecēapod*** (*Beo* 3012). This line can be scanned either with or without stress on *un-*:[2]

/ / / /
gold unrīme **g**rimme gecēapod
gold countless cruelly acquired
[countless gold, cruelly acquired]

/ / / /
gold unrīme grimme gecēapod

EXERCISE: Identifying Rhythmic Stress

With the help of alliteration, word-class, or the position of a word, decide which words in the following lines bear rhythmic stress. Mark the rhythmic stress with the stroke (/).

1) geongum ond ealdum swylc him God sealde (*Beo* 72)
young and old such him God gave
[to young and old (all) such as God gave him]

2 Pope (1966) and Bliss (1967) prefer the scansion with stress on *un-*.

2) sē þe his wordes geweald wīde hæfde (*Beo* 79)
who his of-word control widely had
[(he) whose word had wide authority]

3) ēce drihten, þæs þe hē Ābel slōg (*Beo* 108)
eternal Lord because he Abel slew
[the eternal Lord (avenged the killing) because he slew Abel]

4) þā wæs æfter wiste wōp up āhafen (*Beo* 128)
then was after feasting cry up raised
[then after the feasting a cry was raised up]

5) mǣre þēoden mondrēamum from (*Beo* 1715)
notorious prince man-joys from
[the notorious prince (turned) from human joys]

3.2 Syllable and Foot

3.2.1 Syllable Length

As we saw above, rhythmic stress normally falls on stress-words and occasionally on particles and proclitics under certain conditions. The assignment of rhythmic stress is not only subject to word class but also to syllable length. Rhythmic stress normally falls on a LONG (or HEAVY) syllable. A syllable is long if it has a long vowel/diphthong or has a short vowel/diphthong closed by a consonant. For instance, the first syllable of *mō-dor* 'mother' ending in a long vowel is long. So is the first syllable of *hear-pe* 'harp' ending in a short diphthong closed by a consonant. Note that a single medial consonant belongs to the following syllable while at least one member of a medial consonant cluster belongs to the preceding syllable. All monosyllabic words, which never end in a short vowel except for a few function words, are long (e.g., *sǣ* 'sea,' *sǣl* 'time,' *frēa* 'lord,' *scēat* 'corner,' *weorð* 'becomes').

In Old English metre, the sequence of two syllables of which the first is SHORT or LIGHT (i.e., ends with a short vowel or diphthong) is often regarded as equivalent to a single long syllable and thus may share rhythmic stress, as in *sci-pe* 'ship' below:

tō scipe fōron (*Beo* 1895b)

to ship went
[(they) went to their ship]

This phonological equation is called **RESOLUTION** and the two resolved syllables are joined with an arc as above. Resolution may be suspended in certain metrical contexts. In the following half-line, a short syllable alone bears rhythmic stress; short syllables normally bear stress when immediately preceded by another stressed syllable:

/ /
on **b**earm scipes (*Beo* 35b)
in bosom of-ship
[in the bosom of the ship]

★ ***U*-apocope**
The equation between a long stressed syllable and a sequence of a short stressed syllable and an unstressed syllable is also seen in a phonological rule called *u*-apocope in Old English: the plural suffix -*u*, which is attached to neuter nouns in the nominative and accusative, is deleted if the stem consists of a long syllable, as in *wīf* 'wives' (<*wīfu*) and *word* 'words' (< *wordu*) or if it consists of a resolvable sequence, as in *werod* 'troops' (<*werodu*).

3.2.2 *Foot*

Now we can tell which word and which syllable of the word is rhythmically stressed in a half-line and which unstressed. The distribution of rhythmically stressed and unstressed syllables in a half-line is not random but highly regulated. To consider the rhythm of a half-line, it is convenient to introduce the notion of **FOOT**, a metrical unit smaller than a half-line but larger than a syllable.

A foot usually has two metrical positions, i.e., the **LIFT** and the **DIP**. A lift is a rhythmically stressed part (marked with a stroke '/'), normally consisting of a long stressed syllable or occasionally of a resolvable sequence (i.e., a short stressed syllable followed by an unstressed syllable). A dip is a rhythmically unstressed part (marked with a cross '×' or crosses '××,' '×××,' etc.), comprising one or more unstressed syllables. A combination of two feet yields a half-line. The foot boundary is indicated by the vertical stroke '|':

/ × | / ×
nihtes hwīlum (*Beo* 3044a)
of-night every
FOOT FOOT
[every night]

× × / |× /
syðþan flōd ofslōh (*Beo* 1689b)
after flood destroyed
FOOT FOOT
[after the flood destroyed (the race of giants)]

The first verse consists of two falling feet whereas the second is divided into two rising feet.[3]

The foot may be made up of one metrical position or a lift alone (e.g., *bearn* 'son') or of three metrical positions consisting of a lift, a **HALF-LIFT** and a dip (e.g., *feoh-giftum* 'costly gift,' *hilde-rinc* 'battle-warrior'). A half-lift, which is marked with a backward stroke '\', most often corresponds to the root syllable of the second compound element but sometimes to the derivative syllable of certain suffixes such as *-ende*, *-en*, *-ra/-est*, *-ig*, *-ing*, *-līce*, *-nes*, *-sum*, and the (historically long) penultimate syllable of Class II weak verbs—thus *murnende* 'mourning,' *sōðlīce* 'truly,' and *scēawedon* 'looked at' serve as feet of three metrical positions.

3.3 Five Rhythmic Types

In Old English poetry, since a half-line must have at least four metrical positions, a foot of one metrical position (e.g., *bearn* 'son') always forms a half-line with a foot of three metrical positions (e.g., *Ecgþeowes* 'of Ecgtheow,' *Ecglāfes* 'of Ecglaf') but not with a foot of less than two metrical positions (e.g., *ylda* 'of men,' *gōd* 'good'):

/ | / \ ×
bearn Ecgþeowes (*Beo* 529b)
son Ecgtheow's
[the son of Ecgtheow]

3 Here the foot boundary is drawn according to Sievers's theory. As we shall see in 4.3, some scholars do not allow rising feet.

```
/   \ ×| /
Ecglāfes bearn                                        (Beo 499b)
Ecglaf's  son
[the son of Ecglaf]

  /   |/ ×
*bearn ylda
 son   men's
[the son of men]

 / ×| /
*ylda bearn
[men's son]

  / | /
*gōd bearn
 good son
[a good son]

  /  | /
*bearn gōd
 son   good
```

EXERCISE: Patronymics

In Old English poetry, people of importance are often referred to as 'son of someone or of some tribe,' such as *bearn Ecgþeowes* 'son of Ecgtheow, i.e., Beowulf' (529b, etc.), *sunu Ecgþeowes* 'son of Ecgtheow' (1550b, etc.), *maga Ecgðeowes* 'son of Ecgtheow' (2587b). Below is a list of names of people or tribes in *Beowulf.* (For your convenience, the genitive form is given as well.) Do they form a half-line with words for 'son,' such as *bearn*, *eafera*, *maga*, *mago*, or *sunu*? Note that *maga*, *mago*, and *sunu*, being resolved, are metrically monosyllabic while *eafera* undergoes resolution to fill two metrical positions. If you think certain foot combinations are metrically acceptable or unacceptable, then look up Bessinger's *Concordance to the Anglo-Saxon Poetic Records* to see whether the phrases are in fact attested or unattested in the epic.

Ecglāf (gen. Ecglāfes)
Healfdene (gen. Healfdenes)
Scyld (gen. Scyldes)
Wæls (gen. Wælses)
Wīhstān (gen. Wīhstānes)

According to Eduard Sievers, the combination of the two feet of various rhythmic patterns yields the following five basic types of half-lines in Old English poetry, which are commonly labelled as Types A, B, C, D, and E. Types A, B, and C have two feet of equal metrical length whereas Types D and E combine a short foot with a long one. In Type D there are two variations, one with the half-lift immediately following the lift in the second foot (D1) and the other with the half-lift at the end of the second foot (D2).[4]

Type A: lift, dip | lift, dip
Type B: dip, lift | dip, lift
Type C: dip, lift | lift, dip
Type D: lift | lift, half-lift, dip (D1)
lift | lift, dip, half-lift (D2)
Type E: lift, half-lift, dip | lift

Among the five types, Type A is most commonly attested in Old English poetry, followed by Types B, C, D, and E in descending order of frequency. Although each type occurs either in the on-verse or in the off-verse with a variety of combinations, there is a general tendency that Types B and C are common in the off-verse and that different types are combined to form a line. In what follows, each of the basic five types are illustrated in detail by instances primarily taken from *Beowulf*, with which the reader might be familiar. Our illustration is primarily based on Sievers's classical works with some modifications.[5]

4 Type D2 in our notation is called Type D4 by Sievers, who reserves Types D2 and D3 for minor variants of Type D1.

5 Sievers (1885, 1893).

***Type A**: lift, dip | lift, dip*

A half-line of Type A consists of falling rhythm (lift, dip):

```
 / x | / x
```
bēagas **d**ælde (*Beo* 80b)
rings distributed
[(he) distributed rings]

The first dip may comprise more than one unstressed syllable, most often two, occasionally three, rarely four or five:

```
 /  x  x | /  x
```
wēox under **w**olcnum (*Beo* 8a)
flourished under skies
[(he) flourished under the skies]

```
/  x  x x |/ x
```
ealle būton **ā**num (*Beo* 705a)
all but one
[all except one]

```
 /  x x   x x | / x
```
ræsde on ðone **r**ōfan (*Beo* 2690a)
rushed on the renowned-one
[(the dragon) rushed upon the renowned man]

Note, on the other hand, that the final dip never has more than one syllable. This is also the case with Types C and D1 to be discussed below.

Either the first or the second lift (or both) may fall on the resolved sequence of a short stressed syllable and an unstressed syllable:

```
  /  x|  / x
```
sceaþena **þ**rēatum (*Beo* 4b)
enemies' from-troops
[from troops of enemies]

```
 /  x   x |  / x
```
māþðum for **m**etode (*Beo* 169a)

treasure for God
[(he was not allowed to approach) the treasure because of God]

/ × ×| / ×
hæleð under **h**eofenum (*Beo* 52a)
men under heavens
[men under the heavens]

Consider the following half-lines that consist solely of a compound or a derivative. A hyphen is inserted between elements:

/ ×| / ×
hilde-wǣpnum (*Beo* 39a)
[(with) battle-weapons]

/ × | / ×
ēadig-līce (*Beo* 100a)
[happily]

As there is no single foot of four metrical positions in Sievers's theory, these half-lines are divided into two falling feet (i.e., *hilde*- and -*wǣpnum*; *ēadig*- and -*līce*) where the root syllables of the second compound element (-*wǣpnum*) and of the derivative suffix (-*līce*) bear primary rhythmic stress.

In certain verses of Type A, a half-lift occurs in the position of a dip in either foot or in both. In verse 629a, which has a half-lift in the first foot, the lift in the second foot is short:

/ \ | / ×
wælrēow **w**iga (*Beo* 629a)
deadly-fierce warrior
[the warrior fierce in battle]

/ ×| / \
Grendles **g**ūðcræft (*Beo* 127a)
Grendel's war-craft
[Grendel's war-strength]

/ \ | / \
brēosthord **b**lōdrēow (*Beo* 1719a)
breast-hoard blood-fierce
[the breast-hoard (grew) blood-thirsty]

This variety of Type A is commonly labelled Type A2 so as to distinguish it from the basic type labelled Type A1. Because of their metrical heaviness, half-lines of Type A2 normally show double alliteration and are accordingly restricted to the on-verse.

In Type A, the first lift can be suppressed so that alliteration falls only on the second lift:

x   x | / x
Ēow hēt **s**ecgan (*Beo* 391a)
you ordered say
[(He) ordered (me) to tell you]

x x x | / x
Đā wæs on **b**urgum (*Beo* 53a)
then was in strongholds
[Then was in the strongholds]

This type of half-line is labelled A3. In Type A3, the number of unstressed syllables before the second lift is at least two, often exceeding three as if to compensate for the absence of lift. (Verses with only one [primary] lift are sometimes called **LIGHT VERSES**, and those with two lifts and those with two lifts and a half-lift **NORMAL VERSES** and **HEAVY VERSES** respectively.) As alliteration occurs only in the lift of its second foot, Type A3 is naturally restricted to the on-verse. In addition, A3 half-lines very often come at the beginning of clauses or sentences (see 6.5.3).[6]

Two Lifts or One Lift?

As he requires a half-line to have two lifts, Sievers regards the pronoun *hī* 'they' as forming a lift in the on-verse below:

/ / / /
Hī hyne þā ætb**ǣ**ron tō **b**rimes faroðe (*Beo* 28)
they him then carried to of-sea current
[They then carried him to the current of the sea]

Since non-alliterating first lifts usually consist of weakly stressed elements like *hī*, a majority of scholars today prefer the idea that on-verses like 28a contain only a single lift with the first lift suppressed. Pope (1966), who

6 See Stanley (1974, 1992) and Donoghue (2006).

attempts to account for Old English metre in terms of musical notations, assumes that in Type A3 the harp was struck in place of the suppressed initial lift.

Type B: dip, lift | dip, lift

In Type B, a half-line reiterates the rising rhythm (dip, lift):

x / |x /
ond **H**alga til (*Beo* 61b)
and Halga good
[and good Halga]

Either the first or the second lift falls on a resolvable sequence. Only rarely are both lifts resolved:

x / |x /
ond **h**æleþa bearn (*Beo* 1189b)
and heroes' sons
[and the sons of heroes]

x / | x /
þurh **r**ūmne sefan (*Beo* 278a)
through roomy mind
[through a generous mind]

x x / |x /
under **h**eofenes **h**aðor (*Beo* 414a)
under of-heaven vault
[under the vault of the heaven]

While the first dip can have a flexible number of unstressed syllables, the second dip normally contains one or two:

x x x x / | x /
swylce hīe æt **F**innes hām (*Beo* 1156a)
such they at Finn's home
[such as they (could find) in Finn's home]

x x x xx / |x x /
syþðan hē hire folmum æthrān (*Beo* 722b)

since he her with-hands touched
[after he touched it (=the door) with his hands]

Type C: dip, lift | lift, dip

A half-line of Type C consists of two different rhythms, rising and falling, which result in a clashing of two lifts. As in Type B, the verse-initial dip can contain a varying number of unstressed syllables whereas as in Types A and D1, the verse-final dip never contains more than one unstressed syllable:

× / | / ×
ge**būn** hæfdon (*Beo* 117b)
occupied had
[(they) had occupied (the hall)]

× × / | / ×
þonne **wīg** cume (*Beo* 23b)
when war come
[when war comes]

In this type, resolution is usually found in the first lift, and only rarely in the second or in both:

× × / | / ×
ond tō **fæder** fæþmum (*Beo* 188a)
and to father's embraces
[in the embraces of the Father]

×× / | / ×
Hē on **weg** losade (*Beo* 2096b)
he on way escaped
[He escaped away]

× / | / ×
tō **scypon** feredon (*Beo* 1154b)
to ships carried
[(they) carried (all the goods) to (their) ships]

In Type C, a short syllable often occupies the second lift, which is immediately preceded by the first lift:

```
x  /  |/ x
in geārdagum                                              (Beo 1b)
in yore-days
[in days of yore]
```

As this instance shows, the second lift of Type C often corresponds to the secondary word-stress of a second compound element. Likewise, the 'secondary' word-stress of important derivative and formative syllables bears the second lift of Type C:

```
x    x / | / x
ond gefrætwade                                            (Beo 96a)[7]
and  adorned
[and (He) adorned (the corners of the earth)]
```

```
x  x / | /  x
tō gefremmanne                                            (Beo 174b)
to do
[to do]
```

***Type D**: lift | lift, half-lift, dip (D1)*
lift | lift, dip, half-lift (D2)

As is noticeable from the instances below, the second foot of Types D1 and D2 (especially the former) often consists of a single word, either a compound or a word with a formative or derivative syllable:

```
      /  |  /  \ x
D1: frēan  Scyldinga                                      (Beo 500b)
    lord   Scyldings'
    [the lord of the Scyldings]
```

```
      /   |  / x \
D2: wēold  wīdeferhð                                      (Beo 702a)
    ruled  for-a-long-time
    [(He) has ever ruled (mankind)]
```

While the verse-final dip of D1 does not consist of more than one unstressed

7 Russom (2002a: 315) questions rhythmic stress on the short medial syllable of Class II weak verbs.

syllable, the non-verse-final dip of D2 may contain two unstressed syllables:

/ |/ × × \
sēon **s**ibbegedriht (*Beo* 387a)
see related-band
[(summon) a band of kinsman to see (me)]

In Types D1 and D2, either the first or the second lift (or rarely both) may be resolved:

/ | / \ ×
sele Hrōðgāres (*Beo* 826b) D1
hall Hrothgar's
[the hall of Hrothgar]

/ | / \ ×
heall **h**eorudrēorc (*Beo* 487a) D1
hall with-sword-gore
[the hall (drenched) with sword-gore]

/ | / \ ×
hladen **h**erewǣdum (*Beo* 1897a) D1
loaded with-battle-garments
[loaded with battle-garments]

/ | / × \
micel **m**orgenswēg (*Beo* 129a) D2
great morning-cry
[a great morning-cry]

/ | / × \
wlanc **W**edera lēod (*Beo* 341a) D2
brave Weder-Geats' lord
[the brave lord of the Weder-Geats]

/ | / × \
cyning æþelum gōd (*Beo* 1870b) D2[8]
king with-nobilities good
[the excellent king with noble lineages]

8 Bliss (1967) scans this verse as Type E (3E2 in his notation).

In Type D1, the half-lift may consist of a short syllable alone since it immediately follows the second lift. (Resolution tends to be avoided in the half-lift of Types D1, D2, and E.) Likewise, as it is next to the first lift, a short second lift may occur:

/ | / \ x
scearp scyldwiga (*Beo* 288a)
shrewd shield-warrior
[the shrewd shield-warrior]

/ | / \ x
þēodcyninga (*Beo* 2a)
[of the people's kings]

Types D1 and D2 may be 'expanded' with one (or, rarely, more than one) unstressed syllable after the first lift. An asterisk added to the letter 'D' indicates a half-line of this subtype:

/ x | / \ x
sīde sǣnæssas (*Beo* 223a) D*1
wide sea-capes
[wide headlands]

/ x | / x \
lēoda landgeweorc (*Beo* 938a) D*2
people's stronghold
[the stronghold of the people]

These expanded Type D half-lines require double alliteration because of their metrical heaviness.

Type E: *lift, half-lift, dip | lift*

This type is, as it were, a mirror image of Type D2, often comprising a three-syllable compound or a three-syllable word with derivatives/formatives in the first foot:

/ \ x | /
healærna mǣst (*Beo* 78a)
of-hall-buildings greatest
[the greatest of hall-buildings]

/ \ x| /
murnende **m**ōd (*Beo* 50a)
mourning mood
[(their) mind (was) mourning]

The first or the second lift (or rarely both) may be resolved:

/ \ x| /
wlītebeorhtne **w**ang (*Beo* 93a)
beautiful plain
[a beautiful plain]

/ \ x | /
wyrmcynnes **f**ela (*Beo* 1425b)
of-serpent-race many
[many of a race of serpents]

/ \ x| /
nicorhūsa **f**ela (*Beo* 1411b)
of-water-monsters' abodes many
[many of water-monsters' abodes]

The dip normally consists of a single unstressed syllable but occasionally of two unstressed syllables:

/ \ x x| /
wīnærnes ge**w**eald (*Beo* 654a)
of-wine-hall control
[power over the wine-hall]

Certain half-lines may be ambiguous between Types D and E when they consist of three different rhythmically stressable words.[9] Consider the half-line below:

Fyrst **f**orð gewāt (*Beo* 210a)
time forth went
[Time went forth]

9 Cable (1972) merges Type D2 into Type E to simplify Sievers's five types.

This half-line could be analysed as Type D2 with the lift on *fyrst* 'time' and *forð* 'forth' or Type E with the lift on *fyrst* and *-wāt* 'went.' In verse 210a, however, the occurrence of double alliteration between *fyrst* and *forð* lends support to the former analysis. If there is only a single alliteration, the syntax and semantics of the half-line might afford a clue:

stīg under læg (*Beo* 2213b)
path under lay
[beneath lay a path]

gomel swyrd geteāh (*Beo* 2610b)
ancient sword drew
[(he) drew an ancient sword]

Verse 2213b is more likely to be of Type D2 since the verb *læg* 'lay' and its adverbial modifier *under* 'under' have a closer syntactic tie than the noun *stīg* 'path' and the adverb do. It is, on the other hand, advisable to make a Type E analysis of verse 2610b, in which the adjective *gomel* and the noun *swyrd* form a single constituent. There are, however, certain controversial cases where alliteration and syntax are in discord. In the verse below from the *Wanderer*, while alliteration points to the Type D*2 analysis, the genitive modifier *hrūsan* and the head noun *heolstre* are syntactically more closely tied—thus leading to Type E scansion:[10]

hrūsan **h**eolstre biwrāh (*Wan* 23a)
of-earth in-darkness buried
[(I) buried (my lord) in the darkness of the earth]

EXERCISE: Identifying Rhythmic Types

Scan the first eleven lines (i.e., twenty-two half-lines) of *Beowulf* and identify which rhythmic types they belong to. You might find it helpful to use 'Some Tips for Scanning Half-lines, with Sample Scansions' in Appendix B.

10 If analysed as Type E, however, this verse is an exceptional form where the first lift is immediately followed by an unstressed syllable. Cassidy and Ringler think that the weak syllable ending in *n* is 'easily slurred in the rhythm' (1971: 286).

3.4 Anacrusis

In the verses of Types A and D, there occasionally appear one or two extrametrical unstressed syllables preceding the initial lift, which are called ANACRUSIS:

x | / x | / x
in **C**āines **c**ynne (*Beo* 107a)
in Cain's race
[as Cain's race]

x | / | / \ x
ge**s**ægd **s**ōðlīce (*Beo* 141a)
said soothly
[(it was) truly told]

x x | / x x | / x
gē æt **h**ām gē on **h**erge (*Beo* 1248a)
both at home and on army
[both at home and on campaign]

Unstressed prefixes most commonly occur in a position of anacrusis but other linguistic elements (e.g., prepositions, conjunctions, pronouns, some adverbs, pronouns) can also form anacrusis.

In half-lines with anacrusis, the two lifts tend to alliterate, and most examples are accordingly restricted to the on-verse. In late poems like the *Battle of Maldon,* however, Type A with anacrusis often occurs in the off-verse with a single alliteration.[11]

Although it begins with a lift, a Type E verse normally does not allow anacrusis.[12] Why is anacrusis attested in Types A and D but not in Type E? A clue can be found in the position of the syntactic break within a verse, which shows an interesting correlation with the occurrence of anacrusis.[13] (Note that the syntactic break in a verse does not necessarily correspond

11 *Mald* 11b, 32b, 55b, 72b, etc.

12 In *Beowulf*, there occur nine possible instances of Type E with anacrusis (501b, 662a, 932b, 949b, 1236a, 1329b, 1830b, 1941b, 2441a). Bliss, however, takes them as Type B 'since disyllabic anacrusis is exceedingly rare, and trisyllabic anacrusis unparalleled' (1967: § 50).

13 Bliss (1967: § 46).

to the boundary between two feet.) Anacrusis is common in Type A when the break occurs toward the beginning of the verse (the double vertical strokes '||' stand for the syntactic boundary):

x / x x / x
ge**wē**old || his ge**w**itte (*Beo* 2703a)
controlled his intellect
[(he) controlled his senses]

x / x x / x
in **m**ǣgþa || gehw**ǣ**re (*Beo* 25a)
in of-nations any
[in any of nations]

Notice that without anacrusis the two syntactic groups are not equal in size: the first one (i.e., *-wēold* and *mǣgþa*) is shorter than the second (i.e., *his gewitte* and *gehwǣre* respectively). On the other hand, anacrusis is very rare in *Beowulf* when the two groups are of equal length. It follows that the use of anacrusis helps to compensate for the relative metrical brevity of the first syntactic group and thereby to maintain balance between the two groups. This provides an explanation of why anacrusis appears in Type D, which has the shorter first foot or group, but not in Type E: in the latter, the longer first foot or group removes the necessity of adding anacrusis before it.

3.5 Hypermetric Verses

In Old English poetry, there occur HYPERMETRIC VERSES containing more than two feet and four metrical positions, as below:

/ x x | / x | / x
gān under **g**yldnum **b**ēage (*Beo* 1163a)
walk under golden circlet
[(she came forth) walking with a golden circlet worn]

In *Beowulf*, there occur twenty-three hypermetric verses including this instance, most of which appear in sequence. Verse 1163a above is the beginning of a sequential cluster continuing up to 1168b. Two other clusters are attested in 1705a–7b and 2995a–6b, while there are two apparent instances of a hypermetric verse in isolation (e.g., 2173a and 2297a). Extended verses of this type are much more frequently found in the *Dream of the Rood*, *Judith*, and so-called gnomic poems.

When they occur in the on-verse, hypermetric verses have a normal two-foot verse (most frequently of Type A) preceded by an additional falling foot, as in the instance given above. The lift of the extra foot normally participates in alliteration. Hypermetric off-verses are, on the other hand, normally formed by adding a relatively long sequence of unstressed syllables to a normal two-foot verse (usually of Type A):

x x x x x | / x | / x
gehwylc hiora his ferhþe trēowde (*Beo* 1166b)
each of-them his spirit trusted
[each of them trusted his spirit]

Hypermetric verses are closely tied to speech, being often attested in a group before a speech, within a speech, and in between speeches. They may also occur at the beginning of a poem (e.g., *Max I* 1–6; *Max II* 1–4) or at the end (e.g., *Jud* 337–49; *Wan* 111–15). The use of hypermetric verses might give particular solemnity or importance to the passages or achieve the effect of slowing down the narrative movement, but the exact functions of hypermetricity still remain to be explained.

EXERCISE: Hypermetric Verses

Scan the following hypermetric verses, which occur in clusters in the *Dream of the Rood*. Read *blēom* 'colour' (dat.pl.) in 22a expanded as disyllabic, i.e., *blēo-um*:

swǣtan on þā swīðran healfe. Eall ic wæs mid sorgum gedrēfed,
forht ic wæs for þǣre fægran gesyhðe. Geseah ic þæt fūse bēacen
wendan wǣdum ond blēom; hwīlum hit wæs mid wǣtan bestēmed,
beswyled mid swātes gange, hwīlum mid since gegyrwed. (*Dream* 20–3)

[(The cross began) to bleed on the right side. I was all troubled with sorrows, I was afraid because of the fair sight. I saw the shining sign change in garments and colours; now it was made wet with moisture, drenched with the flow of blood, now adorned with treasure.]

References and Suggestions for Further Reading

While the metrical analysis presented in this chapter is primarily based on the Sievers-Bliss system, there has been another competing theory initiated by Heusler (1925, 1943), and continued in the work of Pope (1966), Creed (1966, 1982, 1990), Nist (1967), and Hieatt (1972), among others. Obst (1987) departs more radically from Sievers, proposing four basic types, which allows many verses of three feet. For the alternative analyses of Sievers's Types B and C, see 4.3.

Stress-words, Particles, and Proclitics: The classification of words in verse according to stressability is based on Kuhn (1933). A critical summary of his classification can be found in Momma (1997: chapter 3). For the post-positioning of prepositions in Old English poetry, see Lapidge (2006).

Foot: Although some scholars (e.g., Hutcheson 1995) find the notion of foot unnecessary, I retain it as a convenient term. There is no agreement about the boundary of the foot; some metrists think that the boundary should not be drawn within a word (see Bliss 1967). Bliss replaces foot by 'breath-group,' which roughly corresponds to syntactic grouping.

Basic Rhythmic Types: For the five types, see Sievers (1885, 1893). Although English translations of these works in German have not been available, there are convenient summaries of Sievers's types and subtypes in Cassidy and Ringler (1971).

Anacrusis: The relationship between the occurrence of anacrusis and the position of a syntactic break is discussed in detail by Bliss (1967: §§ 46–50). For criticism of Bliss's constraint on anacrusis, see Hutcheson (1995: chapter 4, esp. p. 107, n. 33). For the treatment of exceptional occurrences of off-verses with anacrusis in *Beowulf*, see Donoghue (1987a) and Suzuki (1995c: 159–63).

Hypermetric Verses: For hypermetric verses, see Timmer (1952), Pope (1966), Hieatt (1969, 1974, 1980), Bliss (1972), Zehnder (2000), and Ogura (2009).

4 Rhythm: Advanced Topics

Overview

In the previous chapter, we saw that the rhythm of Old English poetry is highly systematic, yielding the five basic types. We begin with the 'Four-syllable Principle,' which each half-line must follow to fit into any of the legitimate types. There are apparently a number of verses which seem not to suit any of Sievers's five types or to observe a proper syllable count. Most of these apparent exceptions can, however, be accommodated to normal verses by reference to the phonological processes of contraction, parasiting, syncopation, and resolution, each of which may add or subtract a syllable. While the metrical analysis in chapters 3 and 4 is primarily based on the Sievers-Bliss system, we will also look at another competing theory with special reference to alternative analyses of Types B and C. This chapter concludes by exploring the interaction between rhythm and alliteration in Old English poetry.

4.1 The Four-syllable Principle

In Old English poetry, most half-lines can be rhythmically classified as Type A, B, C, D, or E. In order for a half-line to fit any of the acceptable types, there is a rudimentary requirement that each half-line must satisfy. As each of the four metrical positions in a half-line is occupied by at least one (stressed or unstressed) syllable, a normal half-line must consist of four syllables at a minimum (see 1.3). In *Beowulf* and other Old English verse texts, however, there occasionally do occur half-lines of three syllables, as illustrated below:[1]

hēan **h**ūses (*Beo* 116a)
[the high house]

dēaþwīc sēon (*Beo* 1275b)
[to see a death-place]

A closer look at these half-lines will reveal that they are only apparent exceptions: when the poem was originally composed, *hēan* and *sēon* were assumed to be **UNCONTRACTED** or disyllabic (i.e., *hēahan, sēohan*) so that each of the half-lines consisted of four syllables to give normal verses of four metrical positions. In editions of Old English poetry, forms that need to be read as disyllabic for metrical reasons are often marked with a circumflex diacritic, as *hêan*, *sêon*, for example.

In addition to these metrically adjustable half-lines, there appear to be some genuine exceptions where emendations have often been called for. In the *Beowulf* manuscript, the hero is referred to as *secg betsta* and *ðegn betstan*, each epithet in itself forming a half-line:

secg betsta (*Beo* 947a, 1759a)
[the best man]

ðegn betstan (*Beo* 1871b)
[the best thane]

As both half-lines are short of one syllable, it has been proposed that the genitive plural ending –*a* should be added to *secg* and *ðegn* to give four-syllable half-lines of Type A:[2]

/ x / x
secg[a] betsta
[the best of men]

1 See also *Beo* 25b, 112b, 386b, 528b, 629b, 820a, 1036b, 1180a (resolved), 1264b, 1883a, 2034b, 2054b.

2 First proposed by Sievers (1885: 232, 312).

/ × / ×
ðegn[a] betstan
[the best of thanes]

Other scholars recover the mid-vowel in the superlative *betsta(n)* to make metrically acceptable verses of Type D1 (cf. *betost* in *Beo* 3007).[3] The initial syllable of *bet[e]sta(n)*, although short, can bear rhythmic stress alone as it is immediately preceded by another rhythmic stress:

/ / \ ×
secg bet[e]sta

/ / \ ×
ðegn bet[e]stan

★ Textual Conservatism

Due to the trend of textual conservatism, most of the recent *Beowulf* editors, being reluctant to emend solely for metrical reasons, follow the manuscript readings in the half-lines above. On the other hand, editors of *Beowulf* in general seem to be more ready to emend non-alliterating half-lines even if there are neither grammatical nor semantic anomalies. In chapter 6, we see in more detail how skilfully Old English poets avoid half-lines of three or fewer syllables by means of grammatical devices, suggesting that in Old English poetry the number of syllables in a half-line is as significant as alliteration.

EXERCISE: Half-lines of Three or Fewer Syllables

Consult several editions of *Beowulf* and examine how they deal with the following half-lines of three or fewer syllables in the manuscript. Note that in verse 2139a *sele* (resolved) is metrically monosyllabic:

gegnum fōr (*Beo* 1404b)
[(she) went straight]

3 Sedgefield (3rd ed., 1935), Pope (1966: 320, 372), Fulk (1992: §§ 205, 276), and Fulk, Bjork, and Niles (2008: 174).

in ðām sele (*Beo* 2139a)
[in the hall]

hrēas blāc (*Beo* 2488a)
[(he) fell pale]

4.2 Accommodation of Apparently Ill-formed Half-lines

In Old English poetry, there are quite a few half-lines that do not fit any of the basic rhythmic types and their subtypes. The majority of these verses are, however, metrically adjustable, as in the cases of *hēan hūses* (*Beo* 116a) and *dēaþwīc sēon* (*Beo* 1275b) discussed in 4.1. In what follows, we see how apparently ill-formed half-lines can be metrically accommodated by reference to contraction, parasiting, syncopation, and resolution. Note that these phonological processes are not invoked in some after-the-fact manner to justify metrical patterns but that they are all well-established processes from other contexts.

4.2.1 Contraction

To begin with, let us look at another instance in *Beowulf* where the uncontracted form is metrically called for:

```
x    x x /     /
þēah ðe hē geong sȳ                    (Beo 1831b)
[though he may be young]
```

This half-line ending with two successive lifts does not properly conform to any of the rhythmic types. Metrical irregularity will, however, be removed if versification is based on the disyllabic form of the subjunctive present verb (i.e., *sī+e*), which gives a Type C half-line:

```
x    x x /     /x
þēah ðe hē geong sīe
```

Besides the uncontracted forms, the *Beowulf* poet also uses the contracted or monosyllabic forms, which would have been closer to his own usage:

/ \ x /
nīðwundor sēon (*Beo* 1365b)
[(one can) see a fearful wonder]

In this half-line, *sēon* must be monosyllabic since the disyllabic reading would give a verse of unknown type such as **nīðwundor sēon*: no verse of Type E is allowed to end with an unstressed syllable, nor is this hypothetical verse an attested variety of Type A2. Thus, the *Beowulf* poet might have had the two variants at his disposal, skilfully choosing between archaic (uncontracted) and later (contracted) forms according to metrical needs.

4.2.2 Parasiting

While restoring uncontracted forms adds a syllable to keep four positions in a half-line, there are also metrical devices in Old English poetry to discard a syllable for metrical adjustment. Consider the following half-lines, which fail to fall under Type E where neither the first nor the second lift is followed by an unstressed syllable:

/ x \ x /
wundordēaðe swealt (*Beo* 3037b)
[(he) died by a wondrous death]

/ \ x / x
sincmāðþum sēlra (*Beo* 2193a)
[a better treasure]

A clue to scansion of these verses is the fact that both the words *wundor* and *māðþum* were historically monosyllabic: a vowel before a liquid or a nasal was PARASITIC or EPENTHETIC, as the corresponding cognates in other Germanic languages indicate (cf. ON *undr* and Go *maiþms*); in the course of Old English, a word-final liquid or nasal became syllabic and a parasitic vowel was inserted. If we assume that earlier nonparasiting *wundr* and *māðþm* were the forms originally intended by the poet, the half-lines above conform perfectly to Type E and Type A2, respectively. Editors of Old English texts often underdot a vowel to be ignored on metrical grounds, as in Klaeber's editions:

/ \ x /
wundọrdēaðe swealt
/ \ / x
sincmāðþụm **s**ēlra

As in the case of contraction, the *Beowulf* poet resorts to the later (parasiting) forms as well as the archaic (non-parasiting) forms. Consider the following half-line:

/ x / x
symbel þicgan (*Beo* 1010b)
[(he would) partake of the feast]

In verse 1010b, *symbel* must be scanned with the disyllabic parasiting form in order for the half-line to observe the Four-syllable Principle.

4.2.3 Syncopation

Both half-lines below are metrically anomalous because the final dip of Types A and C never consists of more than two unstressed syllables (cf. 3.3):

/ x x x / x x
meltan mid þām **m**ōdigan (*Beo* 3011a)
[(Not just a part of the hoard shall) melt away with the brave one]

x x x / / x x
Ne seah ic **el**þēodige (*Beo* 336b)
[I have not seen (so many) foreign (men)]

In Old English poetry, however, a short medial unstressed vowel can be ignored in scansion: such vowels, which were SYNCOPATED in the poem as originally composed, have been restored by the scribes in analogy with nominative forms like *mōdig* and *elþēodig*. The vowels subject to syncopation include short medial vowels in open syllables after long stem syllables (e.g., *dōgres* < *dōgo-res*), short medial vowels in open syllables after short stem syllables (e.g., *micle* < *mice-le*), and short vowels in closed syllables after short stem syllables (e.g., *firn* < *fi-ren*; *ofst* < *o-fost*).

Thus, although the short medial *-i-* in *mōdigan* and *elþēodige* appears in the manuscript, it must be ignored in scansion so that the half-lines above can conform to the regular pattern of Types A and C. (A dot below a vowel again signifies that the vowel is to be metrically ignored.)

/ x x x / x
meltan mid þām **m**ōdịgan
x x x / / x
Ne seah ic **e**lþēodịge

EXERCISE: Contraction, Parasiting, and Syncopation

Scan the following half-lines from *Beowulf* by adjusting the syllable count with reference to contraction, parasiting, or syncopation:

1) **m**an geþēon (*Beo* 25b)
[a man (will) prosper]

2) cwæð þæt se ælmihtiga (*Beo* 92a)
[(he) said that the Almighty (made the earth)]

3) **ō**þres dōgores (*Beo* 219b)
[on the following day]

4) **w**ælfāgne **w**inter (*Beo* 1128a)
[through the slaughter-stained winter]

5) **m**orþorbed strēd (*Beo* 2436b)
[a bed of violent death (was) spread]

4.2.4 Resolution and Kaluza's Law

Like contraction, parasiting, and syncopation, resolution can adjust the number of syllables to fit half-lines into acceptable rhythmic patterns. In the instance below, resolution must be suspended because the half-line would be too short a verse of only three metrical positions with *-locan* resolved (**bắt bắnlo͡càn*):

/ / \ x
bāt **b**ānlocan (*Beo* 742a)
[(the monster) bit into the joints]

On the other hand, resolution must apply to the following half-line, which would not belong to any metrically acceptable type with *-wine* unresolved (**fréowìnè fólcà*):

/ \ / x
frēowine folca (*Beo* 430a)
[noble friend of people]

As already mentioned (see 3.2.1), resolution may be suspended when a short stressed syllable is immediately preceded by another (primary or secondary) stressed syllable. In verse 430a of Type A2, however, resolution must take place even though the short stressed syllable *-wi(ne)* occurs immediately after the stressed syllable *frēo-*.

Why is resolution suspended in verse 742a but not in verse 430a although each of the resolvable sequences is immediately preceded by a lift? A clue for solving this discrepancy lies in the metrical nature of the resolvable sequence itself. The application of resolution depends not only on the existence of the stress immediately before a short syllable but also on the metrical structure of the resolvable sequence. If a resolvable sequence ends with a long unstressed syllable, resolution does not take place: in verse 742a, the syllable after the short stressed syllable (i.e., *-can* of *locan*) ends with a consonant, and is thus long.[4] On the other hand, if the second syllable of the resolved sequence is short, resolution takes place: in verse 430a the syllable *-ne* of *wine* ends with a short vowel, and is thus short. The applicability of resolution according to the nature of the resolvable sequence is known as KALUZA'S LAW. This law, however, allows exceptions in Type B where the resolved second lift very often bears a long ending (*þurh rūmne sefan* 'from a generous mind' *Beo* 278a) and in Type C where the unresolved second lift often bears a short ending (*þæt hīe in bēorsele* 'that they (would await a battle) in the beer-hall' *Beo* 482a). Accordingly, in *Beowulf*, Kaluza's Law is observed in limited verse types like A2 and D1 (cf. *Beo* 430a and 742a above) where a resolvable sequence on the second compound element is immediately preceded by a lift and both are in the same foot. The law is, however, generally abandoned by other Old English poets (see 'References and Suggestions for Further Reading' in chapter 7).

4 More precisely, if the ending of a resolvable sequence is *historically* long, resolution is blocked. Thus, in *gearo gyrnwræce* 'ready for the revenge for injury' (*Beo* 2118a), *-wræce* does not undergo resolution because the genitive singular ending *-e* of the *o*-stem feminine noun originates in Proto-Germanic *-ôz* and is historically long.

4.3 Types B and C Reconsidered

Consider now the following half-lines of Types B and C:

```
 x x  / |x /
Hūru Gēata lēod                                        (Beo 669a)
[Indeed the prince of the Geats]
```

```
 x  x   / | /  x
sē wæs moncynnes                                       (Beo 196b)
[he was (the strongest) of mankind]
```

Some scholars reject the rising foot in Types B and C since Old English words normally take word-initial stress (except for prefixed words).[5] In addition, the Type B and C analyses above result in drawing the foot boundaries in a way which does not correspond to syntactic or semantic groupings but often occurs in the middle of a word or a compound (e.g., *Gēat* | *-a*; *mon* | *-cynnes*). In order to avoid the rising foot and achieve a linguistically more natural grouping, an alternative analysis has been suggested where the foot boundary is placed before a noun phrase or a compound:

```
      |
Hūru  Gēata lēod
```

```
        |
sē wæs  moncynnes
```

As the first foot contains no lift, suppression of the initial lift should be assumed in the verses, as in the case of Type A3. Interesting to note here is that the half-lines above resemble the following half-lines of Type D except that the first foot has no lift:

```
  / x|  / x  \
grētte Gēata lēod                                      (Beo 625a) D*2
[(she) greeted the prince of the Geats]
```

5 See Kaluza (1909), Pope (1966), Bliss (1967), Nakagawa (1982), and Russom (1987), among others.

/ | / \ x
fēond mancynnes (*Beo* 164b) D1
[the enemy of mankind]

Like these Type D half-lines, verses 669a and 196b would have the second foot where the rhythmic stress on *lēod* and *-cyn(nes)* becomes subordinate to the preceding lift so as to be demoted to the half-lift:

x x| / x \
Hūru **G**ēata lēod

x x | / \ x
sē wæs **m**oncynnes

It follows that these two half-lines are to be analysed as subtypes of D2 and D1, which, like A3, are light verses with the initial lift suppressed.

The reanalysis of Types B and C as subtypes of Type D, although appealing, is not without difficulties. Although the new theory analyses the rearranged second foot in Types B and C as analogous to the second foot in Types D2 and D1, Type D usually has compounds in the second foot whereas Types B and C more often have word groups. Furthermore, the following half-lines of Types B and C with double alliteration are more likely to assume two primary rhythmic stresses than one primary stress with the second demoted to a half-lift:

x x / x /
þenden **w**ordum **w**ēold (*Beo* 30a)
[while (he) controlled with words]

x / /x
Oft **S**cyld **S**cēfing (*Beo* 4a)
[Often Scyld Scefing]

Since the analysis of Types B and C is controversial, I use the well-established terms 'Type B' and 'Type C' impartially, leaving open the question of foot division. Hereafter I do not mark foot boundaries unless the topic requires them.

4.4 Interaction between Rhythm and Alliteration

In Old English poetry, the on-verse can be accompanied either by single or double alliteration. The choice between the two alliterative schemes often depends on the metrical structure of the verse. For instance, the occurrence of a half-lift makes a verse 'metrically heavier,' resulting in the frequent use of double alliteration as in verses of Types A2 and D (see 3.3 above).

As we saw in 3.2.2, the half-lift is usually associated with secondary stress on the second compound element or with 'secondary' stress on some derivative suffixes. Although the stress of derivative suffixes is often metrically equivalent to secondary stress in compounds, there is an important difference. Whereas secondary stress in compounds is never demoted to the dip, a derivative suffix is occasionally included in the dip:

x x x / x /
Ne bið swylc cwēnlic þēaw (*Beo* 1940b)
[Such is not a queenly custom]

As the secondary word-stress on the second compound element is never metrically ignored, there turn out to be two types of secondary stress, namely, one that cannot be metrically ignored and the other that can sometimes be ignored, the latter being called TERTIARY STRESS. Constituents that bear tertiary stress are derivative suffixes such as *-ende*, *-en*, *-ra/-est*, *-ig*, *-ing*, *-līce*, *-nes*, *-sum*, and the penultimate syllable of Class II weak verbs.

The distinction between secondary and tertiary stress is metrically significant because it affects the occurrence of double alliteration: a verse with secondary stress in the half-lift position, which would be metrically heavier, is more likely to have double alliteration than one with tertiary stress in the half-lift position.

Tertiary stress is found not only in derivative suffixes but also in certain kinds of compounds with secondary elements of obscured meaning, as in *gār-secg* 'sea,' *Ecg-þēow*, etc. Thus a quasi-compound like *Ecg-þēow* tends to avoid double alliteration (I continue to use the backward stroke for tertiary as well as secondary stress to avoid introducing a further complexity of notation):

/ \ / x
Ecgþēow hāten (*Beo* 263b)
[called Ecgtheow]

/ / \ x
sunu Ecgþeowes (*Beo* 1550b)
[the son of Ecgtheow]

On the other hand, a full-fledged compound like *ecg-þracu* 'sword-storm' tends to show double alliteration when it occurs with another stress-word, as in the expanded Type D1 verse below:

/ × / \ ×
atole ecgþræce (*Beo* 596a)
[a dreadful sword-storm]

Not only the occurrence of the half-lift but also the number of unstressed syllables in a half-line shows an interesting correlation with the alliterative pattern. In Type A, when the first dip is filled solely by an inflectional syllable, single alliteration is common in *Beowulf*; when this dip is filled by more than two unstressed syllables, double alliteration becomes more frequent:[6]

/ × / ×
māga rīce (*Beo* 1853a)
[the kingdom of kinsmen]

/ × × / ×
folce tō frōfre (*Beo* 14a)
[(whom God sent) to people as a consolation]

/ × × × / ×
wǣpen ond gewǣdu (*Beo* 292a)
[weapons and armour]

In Type D*, in which an extra unstressed syllable is inserted after the initial lift, double alliteration is compulsory:

/ × / \ ×
mǣre mearcstapa (*Beo* 103a)
[a notorious border-wanderer]

Finally, it is also worth recalling that the addition of unstressed syllables before the first lift (i.e., anacrusis) requires half-lines of Types A and D to have double alliteration (see 3.4 above).

6 Suzuki (1996a: 149–58).

★★ Alliterative Rule of Proclitics

Kendall (1991: 108, 119) examines the ways the use of proclitics affects alliterative patterns in *Beowulf*, proposing an alliterative rule of proclitics, which states that double alliteration must occur when the second lift of the on-verse has a proclitic before it. The only exception to this rule is *cwēn tō gebeddan* 'the queen as his bed-fellow' (*Beo* 665a), which is fully discussed by Griffith (2005).

References and Suggestions for Further Reading

The Four-syllable Principle: This principle has been generally accepted among Old English metrists; see, for instance, Sievers (1885: 268ff., 312), Bliss (1962: §15), and Pope (1966: 318–20, 371–2). Keyser (1969a) is among the few scholars who regard verses of three metrical positions as legitimate. For criticism of Keyser's view, see Sledd (1969), to which Keyser replies (1969b). For the importance of the Four-syllable Principle, see Terasawa (2009).

Contraction, Parasiting, and Syncopation: The occurrences of uncontracted, non-parasiting or syncopated forms in *Beowulf* are listed in Fulk, Bjork, and Niles (2008: 325–7).

Resolution and Kaluza's Law: For the original form of the rule, see Kaluza (1896; 1909: §§52, 65). Kaluza's discovery is revised and more precisely formulated by Bliss (1967: §§34–40). Kaluza's Law has recently attracted renewed attention with respect to the dating of Old English poetic texts (Fulk 1992). See also 'References and Suggestions for Further Reading' for chapter 7.

Types B and C Reconsidered: For alternative analyses of Sievers's Types B and C, see Bliss (1967), Pope (1966), Russom (1987), and Suzuki (1996a), among others. These scholars cast doubt on the two types for independent reasons. By admitting a half-line with a single lift and dividing the foot according to syntactic groupings ('breath groups'), Bliss analyses some Type B or C verses as subtypes of Type D. Pope scores each line in musical notation, assuming that two measures in each half-line are to be performed with equal duration or isochrony. As each measure has to start with a beat, Pope assumes a suppressed lift at the beginning of verses of Types A3, B, and C where the harp would have been struck. On the assumption that every possible foot 'mimics' a word with respect to stress pattern, Russom dispenses with a rising foot since there is no word beginning with weak stress (except for a prefixed word).

Rhythm and Alliteration: For further studies of the interaction between rhythm and alliteration, see also Bliss (1962, 1967), who associates the occurrence of double alliteration with the position of the caesura. Although he makes the distinction between secondary and tertiary stress with reference to the occurrence of double alliteration (Bliss 1967: §§30–3), Bliss groups them together, using the symbol 'x' for both of them. For recent studies concerning tertiary stress, see Fulk (1992) and Hutcheson (1994, 1995).

5 Metre and Word

Overview

In the preceding chapters, we have observed two important features of Old English metre, that is, alliteration and rhythm. As briefly mentioned in chapter 1, these two principles are highly relevant to the use of words in poetic texts. In what follows, we shall see in more detail how metrical factors lead Old English poets to choose between morphological variants on the one hand and avoid using certain forms of suffixes, words, compounds, and phrases on the other.[1]

5.1 Preference for Shorter Words or Phrases

Although the number of unstressed syllables varies in a half-line, Old English poets tend to employ fewer unstressed syllables than prose writers. In *Beowulf*, the average number of syllables per half-line is a little less than five while in a piece of Ælfric's rhythmical prose called the *Life of St Oswald* the average length is just about seven syllables.[2] In the following line from the *Life of St Oswald*, the on- and off-verses, both of which would be classified as Type A, comprise eight and seven syllables respectively with anacrusis at the beginning. Recall that in poetry anacrusis rarely consists of more than two syllables and does not normally occur in the off-verse:

1 As noted in the preface, the poets' choice (or avoidance) of certain metrical patterns is not considered to be a deliberate act but an intuitive process.

2 McIntosh (1949: 120).

× × × / × × / × × / × × × / ×
on ānum sylfrenan disce, and sōna þā inn ēode (*St Oswald* 90)[3]
[on a silver dish, and soon there came in (one of the king's thanes)]

The employment of fewer unstressed syllables in a half-line naturally leads to a preference for shorter words or phrases in Old English poetry. In the *St Oswald* narrative, there often occur half-lines of 'personal name + *gehāten*':

Ōswold gehāten (*St Oswald* 2b, 257b)
[called Oswald]

Aidan gehāten (*St Oswald* 53b)
[called Aidan]

Birinus gehāten (*St Oswald* 120b)
[called Birinus]

Cynegyls gehāten (*St Oswald* 121b)
[called Cynegyls]

In *Beowulf*, on the other hand, similar formulae always employ unprefixed *hāten* (e.g., *Grendel hāten* 102b; *Ecgþēow hāten* 263b; *Ecgþēo hāten* 373b). Indeed the Old English poetic corpus provides only a single instance of a half-line of the form 'personal name + *gehāten*' (*Hǣlend gehāten* 'called Christ' *Men* 4a).

Old English poets also prefer a shorter conjunction for 'while.' Whereas polysyllabic *þā hwīle (þe)* occurs only eight times in verse,[4] the disyllabic *þenden* is in very common use (some seventy-five times in the poetry): half of the instances of the longer 'while' are attested in the late *Battle of Maldon*, which shows frequent deviations from the Old English metrical tradition. It is also interesting to see that in the translations of Boethius, *þā hwīle þe* in the prose version is replaced by *þenden* in the verse:

þā hwīle þe hē wile (*Bo* 49.27)
[while He will]

lǣt þenden hē wile (*Met* 11.72b)
[(God) lets (the commands) while He will]

3 The line is quoted from Cassidy and Ringler (1971: 243).
4 *Mald* 14, 83, 235, 272; *DAlf* 21; *JDay II* 83; *LPr II* 100; *MCharm 11* 42.

EXERCISE: *Þendan* vs. *Þā hwīle (þe)*

In *Genesis B* 245, the conjunction *ðenden* is glossed *þā hwīle* in the margin of the manuscript. Why do you think the corrector provided this gloss for *ðenden*?

5.2 Choice between Morphological Variants

5.2.1 Adverbs of Time

In Old English, adverbs of time like *ā* 'always,' *gēn* 'still,' and *gīet* 'yet' have an alternative form with the suffix *-a* (derived from the adverb *ā* 'ever'), i.e., *āwa*, *gēna*, *gīeta* respectively. In verse, the choice between two morphological variants is often due to metrical factors.[5] In *Beowulf*, there appear eleven instances of *gēn* while the disyllabic form *gēna* is attested only twice:

/ x / x
fremmað gēna (*Beo* 2800b)
[attend further to (the people's need)]

/ x x / x
Cwico wæs þā gēna (*Beo* 3093b)
[(he) was then still alive]

The use of disyllabic *gēna* is metrically motivated: without *-a*, verse 2800b would consist of only three syllables (see EXERCISE 'The Four-syllable Principle and Word-choice' in 1.4) while verse 3093b would not belong to any of the five types or their subtypes:

/ x /
*fremmað gēn

/ x x /
*Cwico wæs þā gēn

5 This is not the case with *ā* and *āwa*. Besides the unique instance in *Beowulf* (955a), there are some sixty instances of *āwa* (particularly in the *Paris Psalter*), many of which, unlike other adverbs in *-a* such as *gēna* and *gīeta*, occur in verses where the use of the shorter form would be metrically possible.

Besides the two instances in the epic, there occur eleven instances of *gēna* in Old English poetry, in each of which the use of the monosyllabic *gēn* would produce a metrically unacceptable verse.[6]

EXERCISE: *Gīeta* vs. *Gīet*

In Old English poetry, the use of *gīeta* as opposed to *gīet* may be metrically determined. Although the *Beowulf* poet uses the unmarked form *gīet* exclusively, there appear thirteen instances of *gīeta* (including its variants like *gēta*, *gīta*, and *gȳta*) in other Old English verse texts. Consider the following half-lines from the *Meters of Boethius* and give a metrical explanation for the use of the longer *gēta* instead of *gēt*:

1) sumne þā gēta (*Met* 7.3b)
[(Wisdom sang) yet another]

2) næs þā gīeta (*Met* 8.12b)
[(there) was not yet (any of them)]

3) āwēr þā gēta (*Met* 8.33b)
[(not) yet anywhere]

4) Wē sculon ðēah gīta (*Met* 23.7a)
[We must nevertheless now]

5) ðēah ðū hī nū gēta (*Met* 24.46a)
[though you (have) still (forgotten) it]

5.2.2 *Agent-nouns in* -end *and* -ende

When the agent-noun suffix *-end* is used in the nominative or accusative plural (hereafter abbreviated together as nom./acc.pl.), there are two major forms available in verse texts, one in *-end* and the other in *-ende*, the latter being formed on the analogy of the strong adjective declension of present participles. In *Beowulf*, for instance, the compound *sǣlīðend* in the nominative plural occurs with and without final *-e*:

6 *GenA* 2248, 2652; *And* 422, 475; *GuthA* 155, 233, 446; *GuthB* 1270; *Rid 40* 58; *PPs* 93.13.1; *Sol II* 250.

sǣlīþende (*Beo* 377b)
[seafarers]

secgað **s**ǣlīðend (*Beo* 411a)
[seafarers say]

Nū wē **s**ǣlīðend (*Beo* 1818a)
[Now we seafarers]

þæt hit **s**ǣlīðend (*Beo* 2806a)
[so that seafarers (may call) it (Beowulf's barrow)]

The choice between *-end* and *-ende* is not free. In the first instance, the use of the nominative plural form in *-ende* is due to metrical reasons: without final *-e*, the verse would be too short, consisting of only three syllables: **sǣlīðend*.

Among fourteen other instances of words in *-ende* (nom./acc.pl.) attested in *Beowulf*, twelve are compounds occupying the whole verse of Type D1 as in verse 377b above where the use of *-end* would result in too short a verse.[7] The remaining two instances of the suffix *-ende* (nom.pl.) in *Beowulf* appear in verses of Type C with the second lift on the long first syllable of the suffix *-ende*:

× × / / ×
þæt ðā **l**īðende (*Beo* 221a)
[so that the voyagers (saw land)]

× × / / ×
swā þec **h**etende (*Beo* 1828a)
[as foes (have done) to you]

Without *-e*, the verses would be analysed as Type A3 with the first lift suppressed. Note that without final *-e*, the suffix *-end* does not receive any rhythmic stress:

× × / ×
þæt ðā **l**īðend
× × / ×
swā þec **h**etend

7 *Beo* 51b, 245a, 255a, 568b, 1013b, 1346a, 1355a, 1798a, 1945a, 2022b, 2895a, 3113b.

In Type A3, however, the number of initial unstressed syllables is normally three or more in *Beowulf* so that Type A3 verses like those above with only two initial unstressed syllables are rather rare.[8]

Let us now turn to three of the instances of *sǣlīðend*, which are repeated below with their rhythmic types for the reader's convenience:

/ × /\ ×
secgað sǣlīðend (*Beo* 411a) D*1[9]

× × / / ×
Nū wē sǣlīðend (*Beo* 1818a) C

× × / / ×
þæt hit sǣlīðend (*Beo* 2806a) C

In verse 411a, the use of the form in *-ende* would result in a hypermetric verse, i.e. *secgað sǣlīðende*. As hypermetric verses usually appear in clusters, however, there might be no strong justification for the isolated occurrence of the extensive verse here. With the longer *sǣlīðende*, the verses of 1818a and 2806a would be analysed as Type D1 with anacrusis, as in **Nū wē sǣlīðende* and **þæt hit sǣlīðende*. But this rhythmic pattern normally requires double alliteration and appears almost exclusively with secondary rather than tertiary stress. Note also that anacrusis rarely consists of two syllables. Other instances of agent-nouns in *-end* almost always appear in metrical contexts where the longer form would result in metrical anomaly. Thus, in *Beowulf*, the two metrical variants are in almost perfect complementary distribution.

In other Old English verse texts, agent-nouns in *-ende* (nom./acc.pl.) also occur almost invariably in a context where final *-e* is metrically indispensable. Particularly noticeable is that the vast majority of the agent-nouns in *-ende* form compounds to fill a whole verse of Type D1, as in *Beowulf* 377b. While outside *Beowulf* a majority of words in *-end* (nom./acc.pl.) occur in a context where the use of *-ende* would cause metrical difficulties, the form in *-end* does occasionally appear in a context where both forms are metrically acceptable. In the verses of Type B below, for instance, the use of forms in

8 Bliss (1967: Appendix C, Table II). See also Hutcheson (1995: 198–203).

9 Kendall (1991: 246) classifies this verse as Type C (C[1] in his notation) without placing rhythmic stress on the finite verb *secgað*. Under this analysis, the use of the longer *sǣlīðende* would still cause metrical difficulty because the verse-final dip of Type C never consists of more than one unstressed syllable (**secgað sǣlīðende*).

-ende would add only one unstressed syllable to the second dip, giving acceptable verses of Type B such as *hū ðā wīgende hȳra.*

x x / x /
hū ðā **wīgend** hȳra (*Finn* 47a)
[how the warriors (bore) their (wounds)]

x x / x x /
Swā ðā **wīgend** mid him (*And* 1053b)[10]
[So the warriors together]

x x x / x /
and hire **ea**rdend mid (*PPs* 74.3.1b)
[and its dwellers together]

x x x / x /
þæt him þā **fē**rend on (*Whale* 25a)
[(the whale feels) that the sailors (are staying) on him]

The occurrence of the form *-end* in verses compatible with *-ende* can be explained if we conjecture that the shorter *-end*, being the regular or unmarked form of an agent-noun suffix, could be generally adopted unless its use produced anomalous rhythm; the longer *-ende*, borrowed from the adjectival declension, was employed primarily for the sake of metre.

5.2.3 The Relative Infrequency of Agent-nouns in -ere *in Old English Poetry*

In addition to *-end* mentioned above, Old English had two other agent-noun suffixes, namely *-a* (e.g., *hunt-a* 'huntsman,' *lid-a* 'traveller') and *-ere* (e.g., *leorn-ere* 'student, disciple,' *boc-ere* 'scribe, scholar'), the latter of which has developed into the most productive suffix in Present-day English.

While the poet of *Beowulf* very frequently resorts to words in *-a* and *-end* (around seventy and around forty different instances respectively, including compounds), this heroic epic provides only one instance of a

10 Since the second dip in a Type B verse is usually allowed to contain only one or two unstressed syllables, the use of the longer *wigende* in *Andreas* (1053b) could not be metrical. According to Hutcheson (1995: 128), however, *Andreas* provides two examples of a Type B verse with a trisyllabic second dip (cf. *And* 493a, 499a).

derivative in *-ere*, i.e., *lēas-scēaweras* 'deceitful observers, spies' (253), which is a hapax legomenon in Old English and refers to Beowulf and his retainers.[11] Formations in *-ere* seem to be rare in the rest of Old English poetry as well.

In a feast scene in Old English poetry, drinking and music are indispensable elements. In *Beowulf*, a counsellor of Hrothgar named Æschere, who partakes of a feast at Heorot just before being killed by Grendel's mother, is referred to as *bēor-scealca sum* 'one of the beer-drinkers' (1240). Later in the epic, those drinking at Hygelac's magnificent hall are described as *ealo-drincende* 'ale-drinkers' (1945). The first element *ealu* is combined with *wosa* to designate 'ale-tippler' in the *Fortunes of Men* 49. It is interesting to note here that the form *drincere* 'drinker, drunkard' never appears in verse texts. In prose, on the other hand, it occurs three times as simplex and four times with a prefix, i.e., *ofer-drincere* 'drunkard.'

EXERCISE: Harpers in Old English Literature

In Old English poetry, the songs of a minstrel are often accompanied by a harp. Did Old English poets use the word *hearpere* 'harper'? Does *hearpere* occur in prose? Consult either Healey and Venezky's *Microfiche Concordance to Old English* or the *Dictionary of Old English Web Corpus*. For the verse, Bessinger's *Concordance to the Anglo-Saxon Poetic Records* is also available.

Why do formations in *-ere* tend to be avoided in Old English verse texts? Among other factors, metre might be responsible for the scarcity of these formations.[12] Notice first that unlike *-a* and *-end*, the ending *-ere* has two unstressed syllables in succession. As we saw in 3.3, the verse-final dip is not allowed to contain more than one unstressed syllable. Thus, the use of long-stemmed words in *-ere* like *hearpere* and *drincere*, which might have been useful for describing feasting scenes, is highly restricted in poetry; it cannot be used as the second foot of Types A (**mǣrost hearpera* 'the most famous of harpers')[13] and C (**se ealudrincere* 'the ale-drinker'). *Ealu-drincere* and

11 For a detailed examination of *lēas-scēaweras*, see Terasawa (2007b).

12 For reasons other than metrical factors, see Terasawa (2001: 201–5).

13 If the word order is reversed, however, the verse would fit within Type A (cf. *hearpera mǣrost*, *KtPs* 4b).

hearpere could not fit very well within Types D and E, either. Neither verses like **ealudrincere* (D1)[14] nor verses like **sangeres gyd* 'the singer's song' would be metrical in strict verse, where short syllables in derivative suffixes are not usually allowed to bear a half-lift.

Formations in *-end* and *-a*, on the other hand, would be much more useful for the poets in constructing verses of Type A, C, D, or E. The long derivative suffix *-end* is allowed to bear a half-lift in Type D1 half-lines (e.g., *rondhæbbendra* '[no other] shield-bearer,' *Beo* 861a) and E (e.g., *agendes est* 'the owner's favour,' *Beo* 3075a). The agentive-formative *-end* can also bear the second lift of Type C: *wið hettendum* 'against enemies' (*Beo* 3004a). The ending *-a*, which consists of a single unstressed syllable, serves as the final dip of Type A2 (e.g., *Weohstan bana* 'Weohstan (became) a slayer,' *Beo* 2613b) and Type C (e.g., *tō mūðbonan* '[Grendel became] a mouth-slayer,' *Beo* 2079b).

5.3 Constraints on Compound Formation

One of the most significant features of Old English poetic diction is the use of nominal (i.e., substantive and adjective) compounds. In *Beowulf*, for instance, the number of such compounds is so large that on average it occurs every third line, with some 1100 total instances. In this section, we see how the formation of nominal compounds is affected by metrical constraints.

5.3.1 'Prosaic' Here-toga *and 'Poetic'* Folc-toga

An examination of the Old English corpus reveals an interesting distributional difference between two synonymous compounds for 'chieftain, commander,' that is, *folc-toga* and *here-toga*. The compound *folc-toga* is found exclusively in poetry. It is attested in nine Old English poems.[15] By contrast, *here-toga* seems to be quite rare in Old English verse texts. There are only three instances of this compound: in the *Gifts of Men* 76 and the *Meters of Boethius* 1.47, 10.46. Old English prose writers, on the other hand, used *here-toga* very frequently: the number of prose occurrences for

14 Verses of this type are attested in the *Meters of Boethius*, a prosaic verse text: *fēohgītsere* 'the miser' (8.55b) and *woruldgītsere* 'the covetous man' (14.1b).

15 *GenA* 1961; *Ex* 14, 254; *Dan* 108, 527, 655, 724; *And* 8, 1458; *GuthB* 902; *Jul* 225; *Beo* 839; *Jud* 47, 194; *MSol* 119.

this compound is 161.[16] Interestingly, the two instances of *here-toga* in the *Meters of Boethius* correspond to the same compound in the prose version.[17] The occurrence of *here-toga* in the *Meters* could, then, be due to the fact that the poet was following a prose source.[18]

Important to note here is that *folc-toga* and *here-toga* differ in syllabic structure: in the former, the first element has a single long stressed syllable, followed by a second element consisting of a resolvable sequence, i.e., a short syllable and an unstressed syllable; in the latter, both elements consist of a resolvable sequence.

An examination of *Beowulf* shows that while compound sequences with syllable structures like *folc-toga* very often occur (e.g., *cwealm-bealu* 'death,' *ecg-hete* 'sword-hatred, war,' *gūþ-wine* 'battle-friend, weapon,' *hēah-cyning* 'high king,' *sǣ-wudu* 'sea-wood, ship'), those like *here-toga* tend to be avoided. In *Beowulf*, *mere-faran* 'seafarer' is the single genuine exception to the constraint. Other exceptions are only apparent. *Meðel-stede* 'place of assembly, battle-field' (*Beo* 1082), for instance, can avoid the *here-toga* pattern by ignoring an unetymological vowel in the first element (i.e., *meðẹl-*, cf. Go *maþl*). As we saw in 4.2.2, earlier forms without parasitic vowels are occasionally required for the sake of metre. On the other hand, compounds like *worold-cyninga* 'of earthly kings' (*Beo* 1684, [*wyruld-*] 3180) and *fæder-æþelum* 'paternal ranks' (*Beo* 911) have short medial unstressed vowels in the first and second elements respectively, which can be subject to syncopation to produce the metrically acceptable variants *worọld/wyrụld-cyninga* and *fæder-æþẹlum* (see 4.2.3).

Compound sequences of the *here-toga* type are uncommon not only in *Beowulf* but also in other Old English verse texts, whether heroic or religious, earlier or later, most exceptions being explainable with reference to parasiting or syncopation. The religious poems show a higher incidence of *heofon-cyning* 'heaven-king,' which at first glance violates the constraint: neither *heofon* or *cyning* has a parasitic or syncopatable vowel to be metrically ignored. But this compound turns out to be a systematic exception; as a parasitic vowel often arises before a nasal or liquid, the unstressed vowel

16 I exclude *her-togan* and *her-togen*, both of which consist of metrically acceptable sequences.

17 *Bo* 7.12; 46.22.

18 The *Meters* poet, on the other hand, makes occasional alternations to the prose source for the sake of metre, cf. 5.1, 6.1.3, 6.2, 6.3.

of *heofon* could be regarded as 'pseudo-parasitic,' making *heofon-cyning* (with the pseudo-parasitic vowel ignored) metrically equivalent to *folc-toga.*

Returning to the sharp distributional contrast between the two compounds for 'chieftain,' we can now reason that Old English poets might have avoided *here-toga* and instead coined the metrically acceptable alternative *folc-toga*. On the other hand, Old English prose writers, who were not subject to the constraint, were able to make full and free use of *here-toga.*

5.3.2 Hilde- *and* Hild-*compounds*

In verse, the second elements of a resolvable sequence tend to avoid forming compounds not only with the first elements of a resolvable sequence but also with those of a long stressed syllable followed by an unstressed syllable. For a start, let us take a look at an interesting contrast between *hilde-* and *hild-*compounds in *Beowulf.*

In the warfare vocabulary common to Old English poems, *hild* 'battle' is in very frequent use, both as simplex and as compound. When *hild* forms compounds, there are two variants, *hild-* and *hilde-*, the latter being the earlier stem with the connecting vowel *-e* retained. In *Beowulf*, *hild-* always appears when the second element of the compound is a resolvable sequence, as with *hild-frecan* 'fighter' (2366), *hild-fruman* 'war-chief' (1678, 2649, 2835), and *hild-latan* 'those sluggish in battle, cowards' (2846). Note that *hild-*, which consists of a single long stressed syllable, is metrically equivalent to *folc-*.

In sharp contrast to *hild-*, the longer *hilde-*, which has a long stressed syllable followed by an unstressed one, does not form compounds with words like *-fruma*, except for *-frecan* (2205) and *-gicelum* (1606). (In the rest of Old English poetry, *hilde-* is never prefixed to words of the *-fruma* pattern while *hild-* does form compounds with such second elements.) Although the hapax legomenon *hilde frecan* (2205) appears in the *Beowulf* manuscript, it has been emended to *hild-frecan* by most recent editors:[19] elsewhere the form *hild-frecan* is found (cf. *Beowulf* 2366; *Andreas* 126, 1070). As the reader might notice, *hilde-gicelum* 'battle-icicles' (1606) is not an exception: it does not produce the *hilde-fruma* pattern with the syncopated *-gicẹlum* assumed.

19 Fulk, Bjork, and Niles (2008) underdot and ignore the connecting *-e*. The manuscript reading is, on the other hand, retained by Krapp-Dobbie (*Anglo-Saxon Poetic Records*, vol. 4), Nickel (1976–82), Kiernan (2004), and Slade (2002–3).

An examination of the Old English poetic corpus shows that a metrical sequence like *hilde-fruma* is avoided in other poetic compounds, most apparent violations being accommodated by ignoring a parasitic vowel (e.g., *aldọr-bealu* 'injury to life, death' *Beo* 1676) or a syncopatable vowel (e.g., *æppel-fealụwe* 'apple-fallow' *Beo* 2165).

Although neither of the elements contains a parasitic or syncopatable vowel, *Hrefna-wudu* 'Ravenswood' (*Beo* 2925) does not constitute an exception. This place-name compound has the first element in the genitive plural so that it might not count as a genuine compound but as two words. It is important to note here that the constraints on the *hilde-fruma* and *here-toga* patterns do not take effect when they consist of two separate words such as *holdne hige* 'loyal mind' (*Beo* 267), *dēofla hryre* 'the devils' fall' (*Beo* 1680), *Gēata cyning* 'the king of the Geats' (*Beo* 2356), *brimes faroðe* 'the current of the sea' (*Beo* 28), *sele wunian* 'remain (in) the hall' (*Beo* 3128). Thus, *Hrefna-wudu*, a fossilized noun phrase, is not subject to metrical constraints. Note that Fulk, Bjork, and Niles decompound the sequence and read *Hrefna Wudu*.

Let us now summarize the constraints on compounds discussed above:

Metrical Constraints on Compounds: The compound sequences of the *here-toga* and *hilde-fruma* pattern are avoided in poetic compounds. Because of the constraints, a first element of *here-* or *hilde*-type cannot form a compound with a resolvable second element unless one of the following conditions is fulfilled:

(a) The first element truncates the unstressed syllable, e.g., *hilde-fruman* => *hild-fruman*.

(b) The first element has a parasitic vowel to be metrically disregarded, e.g., *meðel-stede* => *meðẹl-stede*; *attor-sceaþan* => *attọr-sceaþan*.

(c) Either the first or the second element has a syncopatable vowel to be metrically disregarded, e.g., *worold-cyninga* => *worọld-cyninga*; *fæder-æþelum* => *fæder-æþẹlum; hilde-gicelum* => *hilde-gicẹlum*.

EXERCISE: Restoring *Beowulf* 3153a

In *Beowulf* 3153a, which is part of a very corrupt passage in the manuscript, the form … *gas* is faint but visible. To restore this verse, several readings are proposed, most of which attempt to reconstruct a compound. Look at different editions of the epic to find out what kinds of restorations have been suggested. In the light of our compound constraints, can you say anything about the plausibility of these emendations?

5.3.3 Absence of Some Possible Compounds

Metrical constraints account for the absence of what would otherwise be possible compounds. In *Beowulf*, there appear two instances of *gūð-wine*, which serves as a kenning for 'sword.' Poets do not construct analogical kennings such as **beado-wine*, **heaðo-wine*, or **hilde-wine* because these would result in an unacceptable *here-toga* or *hilde-fruma* pattern. The kenning **hild-wine*, without the connecting vowel, although metrically acceptable, is not attested in *Beowulf* or any other poetry.

Old English poets make use of kennings for 'ship' by combining 'sea' words with the second element *wudu*. The words for 'sea' which occur with *-wudu* are *brim-*, *flōd-*, *holm-*, *sǣ-*, and *sund-*, each of them being of the *folc* type. On the other hand, 'sea' words of the *here* or *hilde* type, such as *geofon-*, *lagu-*, *mere-*, and *ēgor-*, never take *-wudu* to denote the idea of 'ship' because of the constraints on compound sequences.

EXERCISE: Poetic Compounds for the Drinking Hall

Words for 'hall' such as *ærn*, *heal(l)*, *reced*, *sæl*, *seld*, and *sele* often form compounds to denote noble dwellings. They may, for instance, take as first element words indicating 'mead' or 'wine' such as *medo* and *wīn*, as with *medo-ærn*, *wīn-ærn*, etc. Make a list of possible compounds for 'mead/wine-hall.' Then check which compounds actually appear in Old English poetry and which do not, by consulting Bessinger's concordance. Can the absence of some possible compounds for 'mead/wine-hall' be due to metrical factors?

Compound constraints also explain the restricted inflection of certain compounds. In the Old English poetic corpus, for instance, compounds like *ende-dæg* 'last day' and *ende-stæf* 'end' appear only in their uninflected forms, except for two instances of *ende-dæge*.[20] The *Beowulf* poet, for instance, uses the forms *ende-dæg* (acc.sg. 637; nom.sg. 3035) and *ende-stæf* (acc.sg. 1753). Inflected forms such as **ende-dagas*, **ende-dagum*, **ende-stafas*, **ende-stafum*, etc., are not attested. The absence of inflected forms like **ende-dagas*, **ende-dagum*, **ende-stafas*, and **ende-stafum* can be attributed to our metrical constraints, since each of them consists of an unmetrical sequence with

20 *LPr II* 112 and *Instr* 42.

the *hilde-fruma* pattern. On the other hand, writers of Old English prose do not restrict inflection of these compounds: twelve instances of *ende-dæge,* four instances of *ænde-dæge*, one instance of *ænde-dege*, three instances of *ende-dæges,* and one instance of *ende-stæfe* are attested in prose.

★★ Reasons for the Compound Constraints

The constraints on the *here-toga* and *hilde-fruma* patterns arise because such compound sequences do not fit well into established verse types. Compounds of the *here-toga* type, which in no way fit into Type B, are not suited to Type C (**þæt se beado-cyning* 'that the battle-king'), Type D1 (**beorht beado-cyning* 'magnificent battle-king'; **beado-cynınges* 'battle-king's'; **þegn beado-cyninges* 'thane of the battle-king'), or Type E (**beado-cyning beorht*; **beado-cyninges þegn*) because resolution is quite rare before another resolvable sequence and also because resolution of a half-lift is very rare. On the other hand, the sequence of the *hilde-fruma* pattern is not suited to Type C or E. The Type A analysis of such a sequence (e.g., *hilde-sele* 'war-hall') is avoided, because a short lift usually occurs immediately after a lift. A compound like *hilde-sele* does not fit well in Type D2 (**heah hilde-sele* 'high war-hall') where resolution of a half-lift is very rare.

5.3.4 Compounds and Syntactic Phrases

In 5.3.2, we observed that syntactic phrases do not adhere to the same metrical constraints as compounds do. What this means is that the constraints could provide another criterion (besides the semantic and syntactic ones) for distinguishing between compounds and syntactic phrases, a problem which has long troubled Old English lexicographers. Note that Old English scribes usually wrote forms separately which were elements of a single compound.

Above all, the treatment of *helle* 'hell' sequences (e.g., *helle duru* 'hell gate') has presented serious difficulties to Old English lexicographers. If the first element *helle* is the earlier stem form, the sequence would be regarded as a compound; if *helle* is the genitive of the later stem form *hel(l)*, on the other hand, the sequence would be a syntactic phrase. This uncertainty concerning the interpretation of *helle* sequences results in much disagreement among scholars. Consider the following lines taken from three different poems where the form *helle* is followed by resolvable words like *bryne* 'fire,' *bealu* 'bale, evil,' and *sceaþa* 'fiend, devil':

hearde ge**h**æfted in **h**ellebryne (*Jud* 116)
[severely imprisoned in hell-fire]

hāt **h**elle bealu, þæt þū mōste **h**ālig scīnan (*ChristC* 1426)
[the violent evil of hell, so that you might shine holy]

þæs þe hēo ge**h**ȳrde þone **h**ellesceaþan (*El* 956)
[because she heard the hell-fiend (overpowered)]

As these instances show, the editors of the *Anglo-Saxon Poetic Records* interpret the manuscript forms *helle bryne* and *helle sceaþan* as compounds and *helle bealu* as a syntactic phrase. Most other editors and lexicographers agree with the compound analysis of *helle bryne* in *Judith* 116.[21] The sequence *helle sceaþan* (*El* 956) is also regarded as a compound in other editions, dictionaries, and concordances.[22] On the other hand, disagreement is found in the treatment of *helle bealu* in *Christ C* 1426.[23]

Our metrical constraints on compounds support a syntactic phrase analysis of *helle bryne*, *helle sceaþan*, and *helle bealu* because they consist of the *hilde-fruma* sequence proscribed in compounds.

EXERCISE: *Helle* Sequence

In *Christ C*, we find another instance of the *helle* sequence, *helle fȳr* 'hell fire' (1269), which some editors/lexicographers (e.g., Krapp-Dobbie, Healey-Venezky) treat as a syntactic phrase while others (e.g., Bosworth-Toller) treat it as a compound. Note first that our compound constraints do not apply to this sequence, which does not have the second element of the resolvable sequence. Observe the line where *helle fȳr* appears in *Christ C*:

grim helle fȳr, gearo tō wīte (*ChristC* 1269)
[the grim fire of hell, ready as punishment]

Which analysis do you think should be preferred on the basis of alliterative evidence?

21 Cook (1889); Timmer (1978); Grein (1861–4); Bosworth-Toller; Clark Hall-Meritt; Healey-Venezky. The most recent edition of *Judith* by Griffith supports my syntactic-phrase analysis (1997: 125).

22 Cook (1919); Kent (1889); Grein (1861–4); Bosworth-Toller; Clark Hall-Meritt; Healey-Venezky.

23 Healey-Venezky takes this sequence as a syntactic phrase while Cook (1900), Grein (1861–4), Bosworth-Toller, and Clark Hall-Meritt give it as a compound.

References and Suggestions for Further Reading

Except for some of my own previous work, not much attention has been generally paid to the interaction between metre and word-choice/formation in Old English.

Detailed discussion of the choice between agent-nouns in *-end* and those in *-ende* is found in Terasawa (2007a). Terasawa (2001) explained the scarcity of agent-nouns in *-ere* in Old English poetry on metrical grounds. For the complementary distribution of *hild-* and *hilde-*compounds, see Weyhe (1905), Sievers-Brunner (Brunner 1951: §168, Anm. 2), Campbell (1959: § 349), Bammesberger (1980), Terasawa (1994, 1995, 1998), and Fulk (2007b). The constraints on compound formation in verse were fully discussed in Terasawa (1989, 1992, 1994). Terasawa (1995, 1998) provided a metrical criterion to distinguish between compounds and syntactic phrases with special reference to the *helle* sequence.

6 Metre and Grammar

Overview

In Old English, there are significant grammatical discrepancies between verse and prose in, for example, the concord between subjects and adjectives/participles, the declension of nouns and adjectives, the use of multiple negation, the ratio of case forms to prepositional phrases, and word order. This chapter demonstrates some peculiarities of verse grammar and explains why they might arise by reference to interaction between verse grammar and the metrical principles described in the previous chapters.

6.1 Nouns and Adjectives

6.1.1 Concord between Subject and Adjective/Participle

When the subject is plural, the adjective/participle can be uninflected or inflected with the ending in *-e* (generalized for all genders). Both in prose and in poetry, inflected forms seem to be the norm, but in the latter uninflected forms occur especially when the adjective/participle is placed away from the subject it governs. In the following passage from *Elene*,

þǣr *hīe* in wylme nū
drēogaþ dēaðcwale in dracan fæðme,
þēostrum *forþylmed* (*El* 764b–6a)

[there now in the surging fire they endure the agony of death in the dragon's embrace, enveloped with darkness] the past participle form of *forþylman* 'envelop' does not take the ending *-e* in concord with the plural subject (*hīe* 'they'), which is placed three half-lines away from the participle.[1] Compare the Type A and C half-lines below that contain the past participle of *laðian* 'summon':

/ x / x
laðode wǣron (*El* 383b)
[(they) were summoned (to the palace)]

x x / / x
þā *hīe laðod* wǣron (*El* 556b)
[when they were summoned]

In the first instance, the past participle takes the plural ending *-e* in agreement with the relatively 'distant' plural subject (*hēo* 'they' in 382b) while in the second instance the participle does not take the ending *-e* in concord with the immediately preceding subject in the plural. These anomalies could be due to metrical factors: if the inflected form were used in the latter, the verse would be of Type A with (disyllabic) anacrusis, which is uncommon in the off-verse: **þā hīe laðode wǣron*; in 383b, if the participle were uninflected, the verse would result in a short verse with *laðod* resolved: **laðod wǣron*.[2]

EXERCISE: Uninflected Past Participle

Consider the following passage from the *Battle of Brunanburh.* Although it refers to the accusative singular masculine *sunu* (42b), the past participle form *forgrunden* 'destroyed' (43b) is uninflected or without *-ne*. Provide a metrical account for the use of the uninflected form:

and his sunu forlēt
on wælstōwe wundun forgrunden (*Brun* 42b–3)
[and (he) left his son destroyed by wounds on the slaughter-place]

1 Note also that if the regular plural form were used, the second dip of the Type A half-line would contain two unstressed syllables to give an unmetrical verse: **þēostrum forþylmede*.

2 Mitchell (1985: § 36) ascribes the agreement/non-agreement of the past participles in *Elene* 383b and 556b to metre without further explanation.

6.1.2 Weak Adjectives without a Demonstrative

In Old English, most adjectives can be declined either weak or strong. The strong declension is used when the adjective stands alone, as in *geonge menn* 'young men' (masc.nom.pl.) whereas the weak form occurs when the adjective is preceded by a determiner such as a demonstrative (e.g., *se geonga man* 'the young man') or a possessive (e.g., *mīn geonga frēond* 'my young friend'). This rule is, however, somewhat relaxed in the poetry. Consider the following half-line from *Beowulf*:

brāde rīce (*Beo* 2207b)
[the broad kingdom]

In this instance, the adjective *brāde* is declined weak even though it does not follow a demonstrative. In prose, one would expect *þæt brāde rīce*. The use of weak adjectives before nouns without the demonstrative originated in earlier Germanic where nouns with weak adjectives alone would have indicated a definite referent or idea. Constructions of this sort are much more common in *Beowulf* than in the other poetry, in accord with the generally archaic nature of the language in *Beowulf* (see 7.1).[3]

In the half-line above, the use of the archaic construction is metrically motivated. The demonstrative would add anacrusis, which tends to be avoided in the off-verse (**þæt brāde rīce*).[4] In *Beowulf*, instances of 'weak adj. + noun' occur primarily in half-lines of Type A where anacrusis is normally avoided, that is, in on-verses with single alliteration (cf. 2347a below), in on-verses with two feet of equal length (cf. 2845a below), and in off-verses (cf. 2207b above).

/ x / x
sīdan herge (*Beo* 2347a)
[with the large army]

/ x / x
lǣnan **l**īfes (*Beo* 2845a)
[(the end) of the transitory life]

3 For the statistics of the use of weak adjectives alone in *Beowulf* and other poetry, see Amos (1980: 111) and Fulk (2007a: 273).

4 Note also that with the strong form of the adjective the verse would be too short (**brād rīce*).

EXERCISE: Weak Adjectives without a Demonstrative

In *Beowulf*, we find instances in which weak adjectives follow nouns without the demonstrative, e.g., *bēahsele beorhta* 'the shining ring-hall' (*Beo* 1177a). Most other instances also form half-lines of Type A2 with the half-lift resolved in the second metrical position (cf. *Beo* 1243a, 1343a, 1435a, 1553a, 2474a, etc.). Give a metrical account for why the weak form (i.e., *beorhta*) is adopted without a demonstrative.

On the other hand, the *Beowulf* poet does employ a demonstrative pronoun with 'weak adj. + noun' or 'noun + weak adj.' as long as this does not cause a metrical problem:

x x / x /
wæs se **g**rimma **g**ǣst (*Beo* 102a)
[The grim demon was (called Grendel)]

x x / / x
Swā se **s**ecg hwata (*Beo* 3028a)
[Thus the valiant man]

x / x /
in **s**ele þām hēan (*Beo* 713b)
[in the high hall]

In these instances, the poet placed the demonstratives *se* and *þām* in the first dip of Types B and C or in the second dip of B.

The use of weak adjectives without a demonstrative, though rare, can be found in verses where addition of the demonstrative does not result in irregular rhythm:

x x / / x
oþ þæt **h**refn blaca (*Beo* 1801a)
[until the black raven (announced the joy of the heaven)]

x x / x /
ofer **e**alde riht (*Beo* 2330a)
[contrary to the ancient law]

In both instances, the demonstrative could be added to the first dip of Types B (*ofer* þæt *ealde riht*) and C (*oþ þæt* se *hrefn blaca*) respectively without causing any metrical anomalies.

6.1.3 Weak 'Man'

In *Beowulf*, beside the commonly used *man(n)*, which is a masculine noun of minor declension, the weak by-form *manna* appears six times, always in the accusative singular.[5] Why did the poet resort to the weak form instead of the ordinary form?

To answer this question, let us observe the following verses from *Beowulf* that contain weak *manna*:

/ x / x
lēofne mannan (*Beo* 297b, 1943b, 2127a, 3108a)
[beloved man]

/ x / x
earmran mannon (*Beo* 577b)
[more wretched man]

/ x / x
ānne mannan (*Beo* 2774b)
[one man]

Since each of the Type A verses consists of four syllables, the use of the ordinary monosyllabic *man* (acc.sg.) would result in too short a verse with only three syllables: **lēofne man*, **earmran man,* and **ānne man*.[6]

In the rest of Old English poetry, there also occur instances of the weak form for 'man' (mostly in the acc.sg.) besides the commonly used *man(n)*. The use of the weak by-form is again due to metrical factors, a majority of instances being attested in Type A verses of four syllables where the use of the strong monosyllabic *man/mon* would not be metrically acceptable.[7]

---

5 In *Beowulf*, the weak *manna* always appears as a simplex.

6 In prose, the phrase *ānne man(n)* is in very common use although an adjective often intervenes. (*Ānne mannan* is also attested in the prose corpus.) Neither *lēofne man(n)/mannan* nor *earmran man(n)/mannan* occurs in prose.

7 *GenA* 2589a; *Fort* 44b; *OrW* 1b; *Wife* 18b; *Husb* 28b; *Jud* 101b.

It is interesting to note that in the Type A3 verse below, the use of monosyllabic *mon* (acc.sg.) would yield an unknown verse type (**Hē sceal þone mon*)

× × × × / ×
Hē sceal þone **m**onnan (*Met* 27.31a)
[He must (love) the man]

whereas the corresponding part in the prose version of *Boethius* (124.16) reads *(lufie) þone man*, resorting to the shorter form. It is thus highly probable that the *Meters* poet's choice of the longer *monnan* would have been guided by the metre.

The following verse contains the only instance of *monnan* in a metrical context where *mon* (acc.sg.) would also be acceptable (*Mon ic ne bīte*):

/ × × × /×
Monnan ic ne bīte (*Rid* 65.5a)
[No man I bite]

The weak form *monnan* (acc.sg.) might be used for purely grammatical reasons. To indicate that the element at the beginning of a clause (the position usually associated with the subject) is in fact the object, the morphologically more distinctive acc.sg. form *monnan* might suit better than the ambiguous *mon*.

★★ The Use of *Man(n)* in Poetry
Old English poets would have used the 'marked' or weak *mannan* (acc.sg.) primarily to satisfy metrical requirements whereas they would have resorted to the 'unmarked' or ordinary *man(n)* (acc.sg.) otherwise, i.e., either in contexts where the shorter form is metrically required or in those where both the short and long forms are metrically possible. The *Beowulf* poet seems to have restricted the use of *man* (acc.sg.) to metrical contexts where the weak counterpart is not permitted, but the single attestation of *man* (acc. sg.) prevents us from reaching any definite conclusion.

6.2 Negation

In Old English, multiple negation or negative concord often occurs in prose. In the following sentences, for example, two or more negatives do not cancel each other out:

and þonne hī gegadrad hæfð, þonne ēowað hē hī, *nallas ne* hilð (*Bo* 61.11–12)

[and when (the earthly power) has joined them (i.e., vices), then it shows them (but) does not conceal (them)]

for ðām ðe þā Iūdēiscan *n*oldon *næfre* brūcan *nānes* þinges mid þām hæþenum (*ÆHom* 5.124)

[for the Jewish people would never enjoy any thing among the heathen people]

In *Beowulf*, on the other hand, multiple negation is somewhat rare. The adverb *ne*, for example, rarely occurs in clauses that contain another negative. The following verse is the only instance in the epic where *næfre* is accompanied by *ne*:[8]

næfre hit æt hilde *ne* swāc (*Beo* 1460b)
[never had it failed (any man) at battle]

The scarcity of multiple negation in verse could be partly due to the poets' attempts to make a half-line 'economical' with fewer unstressed syllables (see 5.1). Compare the corresponding passages between the *Prose Boethius* and the *Meters of Boethius* where the negative quartet in the former has been reduced to single negation:

ne eft þe *ne* geortrȳwe *nānes* gōdes on *nānre* wiðerweardnesse (*Bo* 14.22–3)

[nor (do you) again despair of any good in any adversity]

ne eft tō wāclīce
geortrēowe *ǣniges* gōdes,
þonne þē for worulde wiðerwearda mæsð
þinga þrēage (*Met* 5.34b–7a)

[nor again too feebly despair of any good, when in the world the greatest of adversities would afflict you]

8 Eight other occurrences of *nǣfre* are found alone with *nǣfre* (*Beo* 250) included, which some editors emend to *næfne* (cf. Fulk, Bjork, and Niles 2008).

EXERCISE: Multiple Negation

The following is the manuscript reading of a hypermetric line from the *Dream of the Rood* where *nǣnigum* forms multiple negation with the preceding *ne*:

opene inwidhlemmas. Ne dorste ic hira nǣnigum sceððan (*Dream* 47)
[the open wounds of malice. I did not dare to harm any of them]

Can this reading be supported on metrical grounds? If not, give reasons and provide an alternative reading.

6.3 Inflectional Forms and Prepositional Phrases

In Old English, which is more synthetic (or less analytic) than Present-day English, inflectional forms are often found where prepositional phrases would be expected. Especially in the conservative language of poetry, 'archaic' inflectional forms tend to occur more commonly than in prose. When referring to the word *sweord* 'sword' as an instrument, the *Beowulf* poet makes use of the *mid*-phrase only once in the following verse of Type B:

```
×  ×   ×     /   × ×   /
þæt ic mid sweorde ofslōh                    (Beo 574b)
```
[(it befell) that I killed (nine water-monsters) with my sword]

On the other hand, he uses inflectional forms (i.e., *sweorde*, *sweordum*) eight times to express the meaning 'with.' In some instances the choice of inflectional forms over the *mid*-phrases might be determined by the metre:

```
/  ×     /  ×
dēoran sweorde                               (Beo 561a)
```
[with (my) excellent sword]

In verse 561a (cf. also 586a, 2492a, 2904b), insertion of the preposition would make the half-line metrically anomalous since a Type A verse with anacrusis normally requires double alliteration, and anacrusis rarely occurs in Type A where the two syntactic groupings have the same metrical weight, as in *dēoran* || *sweorde* (see 3.4):

x / x / x
*mid **d**ēoran sweorde

However, the addition of *mid* would be metrically acceptable in other cases:

x x x x x / x
forþan ic hine **sw**eorde (*Beo* 679a)
[because I (will not kill) him with the sword]

x x x / x /
þonne ic **sw**eorde **d**rep (*Beo* 2880b)
[when I struck (the mortal foe) with the sword]

The poet need not have hesitated to add an extra syllable to verse 679a since in *Beowulf* the dip of Type A3 can comprise six unstressed syllables (*forþan ic hine [mid] sweorde*). In verse 2880b of Type B, the addition of an extra syllable in the first dip would be acceptable (*þonne ic [mid] sweorde drep*). Furthermore, verse 574b, the only instance with *mid sweorde*, could do without the preposition (*þæt ic sweorde ofslōh*). Here the choice between inflected forms and prepositional phrases is attributable to the archaic style of the poem rather than to metrical necessity.

In Old English poetry, however, there do seem to be cases where metre would be relevant to the choice between two forms. Consider a passage from the *Seafarer* where the verb *hweorfan* 'go' occurs twice:

Forþon nū mīn hyge *hweorfeð* ofer hreþerlocan,
mīn mōdsefa mid mereflōde
ofer hwæles ēþel *hweorfeð* wīde,
eorþan scēatas (*Sea* 58–61a)

[Indeed now my mind goes beyond the enclosure of my breast, my soul goes widely along with the ocean-stream over the whale's home, (over) the expanses of the earth]

While the first *hweorfan* appears with a prepositional phrase (*ofer hreþerlocan*, 58b), the second *hweorfan* takes both a prepositional phrase (*ofer hwæles ēþel*, 60a) and an inflectional form ((*eorþan*) *scēatas*, 61a). As *hweorfan* is commonly intransitive, it is not likely that (*eorþan*) *scēatas* would serve as a direct object of the verb. The noun phrase appears without the preposition in *Seafarer* 61a for metrical reasons. If it were preceded by the preposition *ofer*, the verse (**ofer eorþan sceatas*) would be metrically unacceptable: anacrusis is rarely associated with single alliteration or with a Type A verse consisting of two syntactic groups that have the same metrical weight. On the other hand, both *ofer hreþerlocan* and *ofer hwæles eþel* are acceptable verses of Type C.

The *Meters of Boethius* and the prose version provide intriguing examples of choice between inflectional forms and prepositional phrases.[9] Compare the following passages:

> Gif þonne hwelc mon mæge gesīon þā birhtu þæs heofenlīcan leohtes *mid hlūttrum ēagum* his mōdes (*Bo* 89.20–1)
>
> [If then any man can see the brightness of the heavenly light with the clear eyes of his mind]
>
> Gif þonne hæleða hwilc *hlūtrum ēagum*
> mōdes sīnes mæg ǣfre ofsīon
> hiofones leohtes hlūtre beorhto (*Met* 21.37–9)
>
> [If then any of men with the clear eyes of his mind can ever gaze on the clear brightness of the light of the heaven]

The poet of the *Meters* uses an inflectional form (*hlūtrum ēagum*) instead of a *mid*-phrase in order to avoid the anacrusis in the off-verse of Type A. In the metrical version, on the other hand, an idiomatic *mid*-phrase can be taken over from the prose version when there is no metrical impediment:

> ac se anwealda hæfð ealle his gesceafta swa *mid his brīdle* befangene and getogene and gemanode (*Bo* 49.2–3)
>
> [but the Ruler has surrounded and instructed and restrained all His creatures with His bridle]
>
> Hæfð se alwealda ealle gesceafta
> gebǣt *mid his brīdle,* hafað butu gedōn,
> ealle gemanode and eac getogen (*Met* 11.22–4)

9 On the use of inflectional forms and prepositional phrases in the prose and verse translations of Boethius, see Sato (2002).

[the Ruler has bound all creatures with His bridle, (He) has done both, restrained all and instructed them too]

In the Type A verse *gebǣt mid his bridle*, metre authorizes the occurrence of the preposition in the first dip where the number of unstressed syllables can be more than two. Incidentally, replacement of the past participle *befangene* by *gebǣt* in the on-verse helps to provide double alliteration on /b/, which is mandatory in Type A with anacrusis. Notice also that the plural ending *-e* (in concord with *ealle (his) gesceafta*) is dropped in *getogen* in the *Meters*; otherwise, the Type A off-verse would have unacceptable anacrusis (**and eac getogene*).

An especially interesting verse in the *Meters* has the preposition *mid* where the prose version uses the inflectional form:

> Þēah þū þā ealle gesceafta *āne naman* genemde, elle þū nemdest tōgedere and hēte woruld (*Bo* 79.32–4)

> [Though you gave one name to all the creatures, naming all together and calling (them) the world]

> nemdest eall swā ðēah
> × / × /
> *mid āne noman* ealle tōgædre
> woruld under wolcnum (*Met* 20.55b–7a)

> [however, (you) named all together by one name, the world under clouds]

Replacement of the inflectional form by a *mid*-phrase is attributable to metrical requirements: the *Meters* poet adds the preposition *mid* to fill out the minimum four metrical positions. Without *mid*, the half-line would result in too short a verse with three metrical positions with *noman* resolved.

Not only does metre affect the choice between inflectional forms and prepositional phrases, but it can also determine the case which a preposition will take. In Old English, some prepositions govern more than one case, most frequently the accusative and dative. The choice between cases is often made on semantic grounds: the accusative denotes 'motion' (e.g., *oþ ðæt ōþer cōm / gēar <u>in geardas</u>* 'until another year came to the dwellings' *Beo* 1133b–4a) while the dative denotes 'location' (e.g., *Ðǣm eafera wæs / æfter cenned / geong <u>in geardum</u>* 'To him a young son was later born in the dwellings' *Beo* 12–13a) although the distinction is often blurred. Consider this passage from the *Seafarer*:

Hwīlum ylfete song
dyde ic mē tō gomene,   ganetes hlēoþor
ond huilpan swēg   *fore hleahtor wera,*
mǣw singende   *fore medodrince.*   (*Sea* 19b–22)

[Sometimes I took the song of the wild swan for my pleasure, the cry of the gannet, the song of the curlew in place of men's laughter, the mew's singing in place of the mead-drinking.]

Although the two *fore*-phrases above show parallelism, the first *fore* governs the accusative (*hleahtor*) and the second the dative (*medodrince*). In neither instance can any significant difference in the meaning of the preposition be perceived.[10] To solve the discrepancy in case assignment, it has been suggested that *hleahtor* (acc.) be replaced by *hleahtre* (dat.).[11] In Old English, however, *fore* 'in place of' is often associated with the accusative.

Here metre seems to be responsible for the variable case assignment by *fore*. If we read *medodrinc* (acc.) in harmony with the preceding *hleahtor* (acc.), the half-line would result in a verse of unknown type with two successive lifts (with the resolved stress on *medo*) at the end:

x x   / /
*fore me͡dodrinc

6.4 Principal and Subordinate Clauses

In Old English, some conjunctions and adverbs have identical forms. For instance, *þā* means either 'when' or 'then,' *nū* 'now that' or 'now,' and *þǣr* 'where' or 'there.' In prose texts, word order is of great help in deciding whether *þā* is an adverb or a conjunction, or to put it another way, in deciding whether a clause is principal or subordinate. As a rule, adverbs are followed by the inverted VS order while a subordinate clause introduced by a conjunction has the SV or S ... V order with the verb in clause-final position. Thus, in the following passage from the *Anglo-Saxon Chronicles* where two *þā*'s are used correlatively, the first serves as a conjunction and the second as an adverb:

10 In their notes to the relevant passage of the *Seafarer*, Cassidy and Ringler (1971) suggest that the the choice between different cases after the preposition might have been made 'deliberately in order to achieve a stylistic effect' (332). It is not clear, however, what stylistic effect they have in mind.

11 Pope-Fulk (2001: glossary, s.v. *fore*).

S V V S

Þā se cyng þæt hierde, *þā* wende hē hine west wið Exanceastres mid ealre þǣre fierde (*ChronA* (Bately) 893.38)

[When the king heard that, then he marched west towards Exeter with all the army]

In poetry, however, these rules do not work: principal clauses beginning with *þā*, for instance, often take the order SV instead of the 'normal' VS:

S V

Ðā se æðeling gīong (*Beo* 2715b)
[Then the noble one went]

In the following passage from the *Wife's Lament*, it is ambiguous whether *þā* should be translated as 'then' or 'when.' Punctuations and capitalizations (except for the initial *Ðā*) are not supplied in order not to force one of the possible interpretations:

Ðā ic mē fēran gewāt   folgað sēcan
wineléas wræcca   for mīnre wēaþearfe
ongunnon þæt þæs monnes   māgas hycgan
þurh dyrne geþōht   þæt hȳ tōdǣlden unc (*Wife* 9–12)

If *ðā* is taken as a conjunction, a comma will be required after *wēaþearfe* 'woeful need' in verse 10b with the passage rendered as 'When because of my woeful need I went wandering, a friendless exile, to seek a position of service, the man's kinsmen secretly plotted that they would part us.' On the other hand, it is also possible to take *þā* as 'then,' thereby putting a full stop after verse 10b and starting a new sentence from 11a. According to this reading, the translation of the passage will read: 'Then because of my woeful need I went wandering, a friendless exile, to seek a position of service. The man's kinsmen secretly plotted that they would part us.'

EXERCISE: Is *Se* a Demonstrative or a Relative Pronoun?

Se is sometimes ambiguous between a demonstrative pronoun (*sē*) introducing a principal clause and a relative pronoun (*se*) introducing a subordinate clause. Study the following unpunctuated passage from *Beowulf* by consulting two or more editions/translations and note differences in the treatment of *se*:

Hē ofer willan gīong
tō ðæs ðe hē eorðsele   ānne wisse
hlǣw under hrūsan   holmwylme nēh
ȳðgewinne   *se* wæs innan full
wrǣtta ond wīra   (*Beo* 2409b–13a)

In some cases, metrical analysis can distinguish between principal and subordinate clauses. In clauses containing an auxiliary and a dependent verbal, if the auxiliary precedes the verbal and does not receive rhythmic stress, the clause tends to be principal; if the auxiliary follows the verbal and is rhythmically stressed, the clause tends to be subordinate.[12]

With this rule in mind, consider the following unpunctuated passage from *Beowulf* with 917b scanned:

x x / x /
Ðā *wæs* morgenlēoht
scofen ond *scynded*   ēode scealc monig
swīðhicgende   tō sele þām hēan
searowundor sēon   (*Beo* 917b–20a)

Although *ðā* could be interpreted as an adverb or a conjunction, the auxiliary-verbal order and rhythm would support the former analysis: as the auxiliary *wæs* precedes the verbals (i.e., *scofen* 'sent forth' and *scynded* 'hastened') and is unstressed, the clause is more likely to be principal, with a full stop after *scynded* and a new sentence beginning with *Ēode*. Accordingly, the passage is translated as 'Then the morning-light was sent forth and hastened. Many a strong-minded retainer went to the high hall to see the curious wonder.'

6.5 Word Order

6.5.1 How Alliteration Affects Word Order

As we saw briefly in chapter 1, the order of sentence elements is subject to metrical restrictions. In the Germanic tradition, which places importance on genealogy, referring to someone as 'son of someone else' is particularly

12 Donoghue (1987b: chapter 3). Donoghue concludes, however, that the poets 'adhered to this convention to different degrees, depending on personal preference' (101).

common (see also EXERCISE 'Patronymics' in 3.3). In *Beowulf*, Hrothgar, king of the Danes, is referred to as *sunu Healfdenes*, *Healfdenes sunu*, *bearn Healfdenes*, *maga Healfdenes*, etc. Although a word order like *Healfdenes sunu* occurs both in verse and in prose, a reversed order like *sunu Healfdenes* is attested only in poetry. The poetic word order allows for a variety of alliterative possibilities by substitution of synonyms for 'son' in patronymic formulae:

Swā ðā **m**ǣlceare **m**aga Healfdenes (*Beo* 189)
[Thus the son of Healfdene (brooded over) the sorrow of the time]

sunu Healfdenes **s**ēcean cwōmon (*Beo* 268)
[(We) have come to visit the son of Healfdene]

bearn Healfdenes; sē wæs **b**etera ðonne ic (*Beo* 469)
[the son of Healfdene; he was better than I]

Since the consonant /s/ is one of the most frequently alliterating consonants in Old English poetry, the circumlocution '*sunu* + genitive' would have been particularly useful.

6.5.2 *How Rhythm Affects Word Order: Kuhn's Laws*

As mentioned in 3.1, words in Old English verse can be classified into three categories according to the degree of rhythmic stress they can bear: stress-words, particles, and proclitics. With these classifications in mind, consider the following verse clause, with special reference to the placement of rhythmically unstressed elements ('Par' and 'Pro' stand for particles and proclitics respectively):

```
                          /          /
Ðē   hē   ūsic   on   herge   ge-cēas
Par  Par  Par    Pro          Pro-(Par)

          /  /        /      /
tō   ðyssum sīðfate   sylfes willum          (Beo 2638b–9b)
Pro  Pro
```

[For this reason he of his own will chose us from among the army for this expedition]

/ /
Sorh is mē tō secganne (*Beo* 473a)[13]
Par Par Pro
[(It) is sorrowful for me to say]

As the two verse clauses above show, particles (except for the displaced finite verb *(ge)cēas* 'chose') are all grouped together in the first dip either before or after the first lift. Note that proclitics do not have to be collected in the clause-initial dip: in verses 2638b–9b, proclitics (e.g., *ge-*, *tō* 'to', and *ðyssum* 'this') appear in the middle-of-clause dip as well.

★★ The Position of Auxiliaries in a Verse Clause

As they belong to the class of particles, auxiliaries normally appear toward the beginning of a clause. But there is an exception to this rule. While monosyllabic auxiliaries (including not only those which are genuinely monosyllabic like *sceal* 'shall' but also those with resolvable sequences like *mægen* 'may' and those with a prefix like *ongan* 'began') tend to occur in the clause-initial dip, disyllabic auxiliaries (including not only those which are genuinely disyllabic like *scolde* 'should' but also those with a prefix like *onginneð* 'begins') tend to occur later in the clause and receive rhythmic stress as a result of displacement from their normal position toward the clausal beginning.[14] Compare the following two clauses where the verses containing auxiliaries are scanned:

x x / / x
Swā *sceal* geong guma gōde gewyrcean,
fromum feohgiftum on fæder bearme (*Beo* 20–1)

[In such a way a young man ought to bring (it) about by doing good action, by making splendid costly gifts while in his father's protection]

oð þæt him æghwylc þāra ymbsittendra
/ x / x
ofer hronrāde hȳran *scolde*,
gomban gyldan. (*Beo* 9–11a)

[until each of the neighbouring peoples across the whale-road had to obey him]

13 Since a Type A verse is not allowed to end with more than one unstressed syllable, the infinitive form after *tō* is to be read as uninflected, i.e., *Sorh is mē tō secgan* (scanned / x x x / x). See Sievers (1885: 312).
14 Bliss (1981).

In addition, there is a tendency to avoid a verse clause that contains only proclitics in the clause-initial dip. The following verse containing a proclitic and a particle in the clause-initial dip is metrically acceptable; the finite verb *(ge)lēah* 'deceived,' which is dislocated from the clause-initial dip, serves as the second lift of Type B:

x x / x /
him sēo **w**ēn ge-lēah (*Beo* 2323b)[15]
Par Pro Pro-(Par)
[this expectation deceived him]

On the other hand, the *Beowulf* poet normally does not resort to Type B verses like the hypothetical one below with an initial dip consisting solely of a proclitic:

x / x x /
*sēo **w**ēn him ge-lēah
Pro Par Pro-(Par)

The rhythmic pattern of this verse is acceptable, but the syntax is not.[16] These observations lead to the following two 'laws,' generally known as **KUHN'S LAWS** after Hans Kuhn, who formulated them:[17]

Kuhn's First Law: Particles must be placed together in the first dip of a clause (i.e., either before or immediately after the first lift).

Kuhn's Second Law: At the beginning of a clause, the dip must contain particles; in other words, proclitics alone cannot occupy the clause-initial dip.

EXERCISE: Kuhn's Laws and Textual Criticism

In line 2149 of *Genesis A*, the off-verse lacks alliteration. Krapp-Dobbie (*Anglo-Saxon Poetic Records*, vol. 1) add *selfa* 'self' for the sake of the metre. Note also that *rīces* 'of kingdom' is an emendation of the manuscript form *rice*:

---

15 Cf. also *GenA* 49a, 1446b.

16 The order *sēo wēn geléah him (scanned x / x / x) would not be possible even under Sievers's system since an off-verse does not usually take anacrusis, which demands double alliteration.

17 Kuhn (1933).

Sodoma rīce[s]; ac þū [selfa] mōst heonon
hūðe lǣdan, þe ic þē æt hilde geslōh (*GenA* 2149–50)

[(ancient treasures) of the kingdom of Sodom; but you yourself can take quickly from here what I gained for you in battle]

Is the insertion of *selfa* between two particles (i.e., *þū* 'you' and *mōst* 'must') justified in the light of Kuhn's Laws? If not, can you suggest any alternative reading for 2149b?

While Kuhn's First Law is rather strictly observed in *Beowulf*,[18] there are not a few exceptions to his second law. Among such violations in the epic are those that contain a demonstrative and/or a preposition alone in the clause-initial dip:[19]

/ /
þone cwealm ge-wræc (*Beo* 107b)
Pro Pro-(Par)
[(He) avenged the killing]

/ /
Æt þǣm āde wæs (*Beo* 1110a)
Pro Pro
[On the pyre was (easily visible)]

In the rest of the poetic corpus, while Kuhn's First Law is generally observed, the second law again admits of quite a few exceptions though the frequency of exceptions varies from poem to poem: *Judith*, for instance, follows the rule very faithfully but in another late poem, the *Battle of Maldon*, breaches often occur.[20]

★★ Alliterating Finite Verbs in the Clause-initial Position
According to Kuhn's theory, since it stands in the normal position for a particle, the alliterating *(ge)feah* 'rejoiced' should not be rhythmically stressed in the following verse where alliteration on the finite verb is regarded as accidental or ornamental:

18 For a few exceptions in *Beowulf*, see, for instance, 1108b–9 (especially 1109b), where the unstressed finite verb *wæs* (particle) does not occur in the first dip of the clause.
19 Kuhn (1933: 44) identifies fourteen breaches in *Beowulf*. See also Hutcheson (1992b: 130).
20 Momma (1997: 73).

/

ne *gefeah* hē þære fæhðe (*Beo* 109a)

Par Pro-Par Par Pro

[he did not rejoice the feud]

In *Beowulf*, however, there occur instances of alliterating clause-initial finite verbs that must bear rhythmic stress:

/ / / /

Gefēng þā be eaxle —nalas for fæhðe mearn— (*Beo* 1537)

[(He) then seized (Grendel's mother) by the shoulder–he did not feel anxiety about the hostile deed]

In order to avoid the metrical anomaly (including the breach of the Alliterative Rule of Precedence (see 2.3)), an emendation of *eaxle* 'shoulder' to *feaxe* 'hair' has been proposed so that the on-verse can be scanned with only one lift as Type A3 (*Gefēng þā be feaxe*).[21] Although this emendation looks appealing, the epic shows instances of a finite verb taking alliterative precedence over a noun.[22]

6.5.3 *Syntactic Classification of Half-lines*

Despite the problems and shortcomings of Kuhn's theory, his laws have been widely acknowledged with modifications among scholars of Old English metre and grammar. There have recently been attempts to reinterpret Sievers's basic verse types in the light of Kuhn's theory. According to the first law, which requires particles to be grouped together in the first dip of the clause, the following verse with one or more particles before or immediately after the first lift has to be clause-initial:

/ /

Swā sceal geong guma (*Beo* 20a)

Par Par

[In such a way a young man ought (to)]

21 See Sedgefield (2nd ed., 1913), Wyatt-Chambers (1920), Bliss (1967), Jack (1994), and Bammesberger (2001). Fulk, Bjork, and Niles also note that *eaxle* in 1537a is '[v]ery likely corrupted from *feaxe* "hair"' (2008: 207, note on line 1537).

22 See *Beo* 1128b, 1137b, 1441b, 1872b.

/ /
Bēow wæs **b**rēme (*Beo* 18a)
Par
[Beow was renowned]

On the other hand, a verse beginning with one or more proclitics alone may not be clause-initial because the second law forbids the clause-initial dip to contain only proclitics without particles:

/ /
of **f**eorwegum (*Beo* 37a)
Pro
[from distant places]

When a half-line begins with a lift and there are no particle(s) in its first dip, the half-line may appear anywhere in the clause:

/ /
Landweard on-fand <beginning the clause> (*Beo* 1890b)
Pro
[The landguard found (the men's return)]

/ /
bēaga **b**ryttan <occurring in the middle of the clause> (*Beo* 35a)
[the distributor of rings]

/ /
mǣrne be **m**æste <occurring at the end of the clause> (*Beo* 36a)
Pro
[the famous one by the mast]

To sum up, on the basis of Kuhn's theory, the following three types of verses can be distinguished in poems like *Beowulf*, which shows relatively strict observance of the second law as well as the first:[23]

(I) clause-initial verse: contains one or more particles before or immediately after the first lift

23 Kendall (1991).

(II) clause-non-initial verse: contains proclitics alone at the beginning
(III) clause-unrestricted verse: begins with the lift without particle(s) in the first dip

Knowledge of such verse classifications must have been very useful for Old English poets to compose in a rapid and extemporaneous way.

The syntactic typologies of half-lines would also seem to require reconsideration of Sievers's five types.[24] On syntactic grounds, Sievers's Type A3, for instance, turns out to show a closer affinity to Types B and C than to Types A1 and A2 because Types A3, B, and C begin with a dip and are 'clause-initial.' Furthermore, both of the half-lines below, which are classified as Type B in Sievers's theory, need to be distinguished syntactically:

x x / x /
þǣr æt **h**ȳðe stōd (*Beo* 32a)
Par Pro

[There at the harbour stood (the ship)]

x / x /
þurh slīðne nīð (*Beo* 184a)
Pro

[because of dire affliction]

The first instance containing a particle (*þǣr*) and a proclitic (*æt*) is labelled 'clause-initial' whereas the second with a proclitic alone (*þurh*) is 'clause-non-initial.' A syntactic distinction is also to be made between the following verses of Type C:

x / /x
Oft **S**cyld **S**cēfing (*Beo* 4a)
Par

[Often Scyld Scefing]

x / / x
in **w**o͡rold **w**ōcun (*Beo* 60a)
Pro

[(they) were born into the world]

24 Kendall (1991: chapter 15; Appendix 'A Typology of the Metre of *Beowulf* in Relation to the Metrical Grammar').

Verse 4a with a particle at the beginning (*oft*, adv.) is 'clause-initial' and verse 60a beginning with a proclitic alone (*in*, prep.) is 'clause-non-initial.'

Type A verses can be either 'clause-initial' with particle(s) in the dip immediately following the initial lift (cf. *Beo* 18a above) or 'clause-unrestricted' otherwise (cf. *Beo* 35a, 36a above).

The relationship between metrico-syntactic classifications and Sievers's five rhythmic types is summarized in the following diagram:

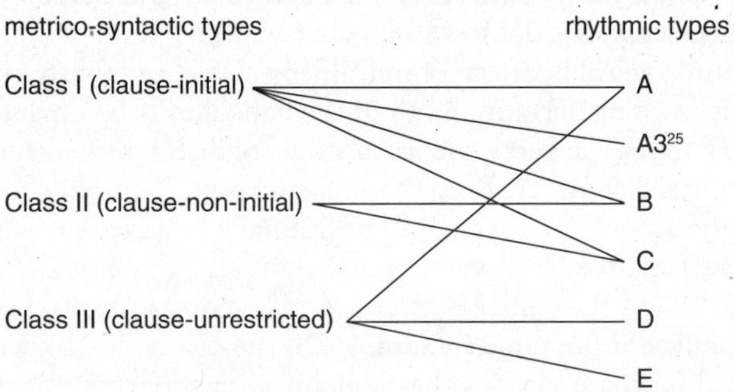

EXERCISE: Kuhn's Laws and Punctuation

In *Beowulf* 1912b–13, many of the editors associate *lyftgeswenced* with the preceding verse, placing a comma after it and interpreting the passage as 'The ship rushed forward, driven by the wind; (it) rested on shore':

cēol up geþrang
lyftgeswenced, on lande stōd.

In the light of the metrico-syntactic classifications and Kuhn's Laws (especially his second law), is this reading plausible? If not, suggest an alternative reading and punctuation.

25 As more than three unstressed syllables usually occur before the only lift in Type A3, it is less likely that proclitics alone would occupy the initial dip to make an A3 verse 'clause-non-initial.'

References and Suggestions for Further Reading

Weak Adjectives without a Demonstrative: The use of weak adjectives without a demonstrative has often received attention in studies of poetic archaisms (cf. Lichtenheld 1873; Klaeber 1950: xcvi, n. 4, xcii; Amos 1980; Fulk 2007a).

Weak By-form *Manna*: On the choice between *man(n)* and the weak by-form *manna* on metrical grounds in *Beowulf* and other Old English poetry, see Terasawa (2010).

Negation: On the scarcity of multiple negation in Old English poetry, see Mitchell (1983, 1985: §§ 1609–13). Yoshino (1978) compares the use of negation in the prose and verse translations of Boethius.

Inflectional Forms vs. Prepositional Phrases: Sato (2002) studies the use of inflectional forms and prepositional phrases (particularly *mid*-phrases) in the prose and verse translations of Boethius, demonstrating that metre affects the choice between the two constructions.

Principal vs. Subordinate Clauses: On the distinction between principal and subordinate clauses that contain an auxiliary and a verbal, see Donoghue (1987b: chapter 3). Blockley separates conjunctions from adverbs in terms of word order, stating that '[w]ords like *þa* serve as conjunctions when they are clause-initial and immediately followed by some sentence element other than the finite verb' (2001: 219).

Kuhn's Laws: In his article published in 1933, Kuhn formulated his two laws concerning the placement of unstressed elements in Old English verse clauses. A comprehensive summary of these laws is found in Campbell (1970: 94). Kuhn's Laws have often been challenged and modified: Mitchell (1985: § 3947) notices the dangers of circular argument in Kuhn's theory; Russom (1996) attempts to explain Kuhn's Laws with reference to his word-foot theory; Momma (1997), who reexamines the laws on the basis of a more extensive corpus, relaxes Kuhn's First Law while eliminating his second law. Donoghue (1997: 69–75) demonstrates the validity of Kuhn's First Law. Mines (2002) tests the validity of the second law with reference to eighteen poems (excluding *Beowulf*). For further criticism of Kuhn's theory, see Cosmos (1976–7), Hutcheson (1992b), and Blockley and Cable (1995). For proposed repunctuations and emendations in the light of Kuhn's Laws, see Lucas (1985), Donoghue (1987b: Appendix 2), and Momma (1997: 64).

Verse-initial Alliterating Verbs: In scanning verse-initial alliterating verbs, some scholars who value Kuhn's Laws regard alliteration as non-functional/ornamental. They would not assign rhythmic stress to verbs like *gewāt* in *Gewāt þā ofer wǣgholm* '(it) set off across the surging sea' (*Beo* 217a): cf. Bliss (1967: § 20) and Kendall (1983: 7–9; 1991: 22–4). Other scholars treat alliterating finite verbs as rhythmically stressed. See Lehmann and Tabusa (1958: 5–7) and more recently Hutcheson (1992b: 134–6). Momma (1996) takes a middle-of-the-road line.

Metrico-syntactic Classification of Half-lines: For the classification of half-lines into 'clause-initial,' 'clause-non-initial,' and 'unrestricted,' see Kendall (1983, 1991). For criticism of Kendall's metrical grammar, see Lucas (1987). On the basis of the fact that A3 verses very often open a clause, a sentence, a speech, or a numbered section, Stanley (1992: 271–84) proposes several repunctuations in the text of *Beowulf*, although with 'a word of caution.'

7 Other Problems Related to Old English Metre

Overview

In the preceding chapters we have considered Old English metre and its relevance to lexical and grammatical choice in poetry. This chapter will explore other interesting questions relevant to Old English metre, concerning whether metrical evidence could provide clues to the dating of texts, authorship, and the distinction between verse and prose. Since some of these issues are still matters of great controversy, I shall try to maintain as proper a balance as possible among different views and theories, some of which are also referred to in 'References and Suggestions for Further Reading' at the end of the chapter.

7.1 Metre and the Dating of Texts

Most Old English literary texts have come down to us through manuscripts of the late tenth, eleventh, and twelfth centuries. A poem like *Cædmon's Hymn*, which survives in some twenty manuscripts from the eighth century to the fifteenth, however, was composed earlier—probably as early as the late seventh century—than it was copied in the manuscripts. In a *Chronicle* poem like the *Death of Edgar* (AD 975), the composition date would be closer to the dates of the three manuscripts containing the text. But due to the paucity of external evidence—contemporary references to authors and times of composition—most of the extant verse texts are quite difficult to date. Accordingly, some Old English scholars have vigorously attempted to date the poetry by metrical as well as phonological, grammatical, lexical, or stylistic evidence. Note also that the problem of dating Old English verse texts is closely tied up with that of their dialect: West

Saxon traits show lateness (i.e., late ninth or tenth century) whereas Anglian traits point to an earlier date.

One of the metrical criteria for dating is concerned with alliteration between velar *g* and palatal *g* (represented as *ġ*). In Old English poetry, as we saw in 2.1, the two different *g*'s often alliterate with each other:

Hwæt, wē Gār-Dena in ġeārdagum (*Beo* 1)
[Lo! We (have heard of the glory) of Spear-Danes in days of yore]

on þām ġearwum þe his gāst onfeng (*GenA* 1212)
[in the clothing that his spirit received]

ġearwe tō gūðe. Gāras līxtan (*El* 23)
[(they were) ready for the battle. Spears shone]

ġēomor hweorfan. Þām bið gomenes wana (*GuthB* 1354)
[(he must) roam miserably. (There) is a lack of joy for him]

The late poem *Battle of Maldon* (composed after AD 991) avoids alliterating between velar and palatal *g* since the two *g*'s would have been phonologically distinct at the time of composition. In this poem, velar *g* alliterates with velar *g* and palatal *g* with palatal *g*.[1] Consider now the following apparent exceptions in *Maldon* where two different *g*'s alliterate with each other:

/ / /
þæt ġē þisne gārræs mid gafole forġyldon (*Mald* 32)
[(it will be better) that you should buy off this spear-attack with tribute]

/ / / /
Þǣr onġēan gramum ġearowe stōdon (*Mald* 100)
[There against the enemies, (they) stood ready]

/ / / /
Godrine and Godwīg, gūþe ne ġȳmdon (*Mald* 192)
[Godwine(?) and Godwig (ran away), (they) did not care for the battle]

1 For alliteration between two velar *g*'s, see *Mald* (13, 35, 61, 94, 109, 170, 176, 187, 237, 262, 285, 287, 296, 315, 321, 325). For alliteration between two palatal *g*'s, see *Mald* (84, 274).

Since the second lift of the off-verse usually cannot take part in alliteration, however, systematic alliteration should fall only on the velar g's: *gār-rǣs* and *gafole* in verse 32 and *Godrine*, *Godwīg*, and *gūþe* in verse 192. In verse 100, as the second lift of the on-verse does not have to take part in alliteration, palatal g of *(on)ġēan* and *ġearowe* may be assumed to alliterate.[2] It is safe to conclude that palatal and velar g do not alliterate with each other in *Maldon*. The tendency to avoid alliterating two different g's can also be observed in other late poems like the *Judgement Day II*, the *Chronicle* poems (perhaps including *Brunanburh*, which has no unambiguous case of the two sounds alliterating),[3] and the *Menologium*.

EXERCISE: The 'G' Test for Dating

In *Judith*, which is considered to be a late composition (i.e., late ninth or tenth century), do velar and palatal g alliterate? Skim through the poem and find relevant instances. Do your findings affect the validity of the 'g' test for dating?

In 4.2.1, we saw that earlier uncontracted forms such as *hēahan* for *hēan* 'high' are to be posited for metrical reasons in some Old English poems. If a verse text primarily exhibits uncontracted or contracted forms, we might assume that it could be dated earlier or later. In *Genesis A*, considered one of the earliest Old English poems, occurrences of uncontracted forms with intervocalic *h* overwhelm those of contracted forms (twenty-three uncontracted vs. five contracted) while the later Cynewulfian poems contain almost exclusively contracted forms.[4]

Parasiting can also be used as a metrical criterion for dating. In *Genesis A*, the use of earlier forms without parasiting is slightly more frequent than the use of later forms with parasiting, whereas the Cynewulf canon shows predominant use of parasitic forms with only one nonparasiting form.[5] However, the 'parasiting' test sometimes contradicts the 'contraction' test: the former indicates that *Beowulf*, which has far more metrically attested forms without parasiting, should have been composed earlier than

2 In the formulaic phrase *(þǣr) ongēan gramum*, the preposition *ongēan* preceding the noun bears rhythmic stress as in *Elene* 43a, *Juliana* 628a, and *Beowulf* 1034a.

3 See Campbell (1938: 33).

4 Amos (1980: 46).

5 Fulk (1989, 2007b: 307).

Genesis A; the latter, on the other hand, shows that *Genesis A*, with its predominant use of uncontracted forms, should be older than *Beowulf*, which prefers contracted forms.[6] Thus, the choice between earlier and later metrical forms could be due to the poets' individual styles rather than chronological factors.

Earlier linguistic forms are not infrequently attested in late Old English poems. Consider the following verse from the *Battle of Maldon*:

wǣpen ūp āhōf (*Mald* 130b)
[(he) raised up his weapon]

Although it was spelled out, a parasitic vowel must be metrically ignored and the half-line is scanned as Type D2 (*wǣpẹn úp āhōf*). The Type D*2 analysis (*wǣpen úp āhōf*) is less likely since the expanded type usually requires double alliteration, restricted to the on-verse. The *Maldon* poet would have had earlier nonparasiting forms as metrical variants at his disposal even after they were no longer part of his own language. Earlier linguistic features could be preserved in the language of poetry not only through poetic formulae but also by analogical formations on the model of inflected cases (e.g., *wǣpna*). Thus it is advisable to keep in mind that occurrences of archaic forms without parasiting do not necessarily point to early composition of the poetic text where the relevant forms appear. The same caution must be applied when using contraction as a criterion for dating the poetry.

7.2 Metre and Authorship

One difficulty in dating Old English verse texts is the fact that most are anonymous. Indeed, identifying the authorship of the texts as well as the dating has been a major focus of the studies of Old English poetry. Among others, the problem of the Cynewulf canon has always attracted scholarly attention. At one time, a large amount of Old English poetry was ascribed to this poet, but more recently, Cynewulf has been considered the author only of *Elene*, *Juliana*, *Christ B*, and the *Fates of the Apostles*, each of which contains his runic signature toward the end.

If they are composed by a single author (perhaps Cynewulf), the four signed poems must show some linguistic similarities (including metrical practice) unless the author changed his style during his career. As we saw

6 Amos (1980: 46).

in 6.5.2, while Kuhn's First Law is strictly observed in the extant Old English verse corpus, adherence to his second law varies from one poem to another. Among Old English poems, *Elene*, *Juliana*, and *Christ B* are the ones that most strictly observe the second law, which might indicate single authorship of the three.[7] (The *Fates of the Apostles* will be excluded in the following discussion of Cynewulf authorship, as it is too short to provide a sufficient number of relevant instances.)

In 6.4, we observed that in principal clauses containing an auxiliary (v) and a verbal (V), the former tends to precede the latter without receiving rhythmic stress whereas in subordinate clauses, the rhythmically stressed auxiliary tends to follow the verbal. *Christ B* shows a high proportion of the order vV in principal clauses but *Elene* and *Juliana* employ v́V as frequently as vV.[8] In subordinate clauses, on the other hand, the three signed poems adhere to the rule to different degrees, as the following table indicates:[9]

	vV	v́V	Vv́
Elene	4%	27%	70%
Christ B	8%	39%	54%
Juliana	2%	47%	51%

EXERCISE: Cynewulf's Signed Poems

Linguistic discrepancies among the signed poems described above might disprove common authorship, but can you think of any other way to account for the differences?

Tests for auxiliaries and verbals may disclose something interesting about the authorship of *Solomon and Saturn*, the two parts of which have generally been ascribed to two different poets (lines 1–169 and lines 179–506).[10] Both parts of the poem, however, show anomalies in the behaviour of the auxiliary.[11] Unlike other Old English verse texts, they do not

7 Momma (1997: 73, 188).
8 Donoghue (1987b: 58–9).
9 The table is based on Donoghue (1987b: 77).
10 Menner (1941: 5–7) and Krapp-Dobbie (*Anglo-Saxon Poetic Records*, 6: lix).
11 Donoghue (1987b: 104–6).

discriminate between principal and subordinate clauses with respect to auxiliary-verbal order: the two parts show as low a proportion of Vv́ in subordinate clauses as in principal clauses, and such a trait is not attested in any other poem. The metrico-grammatical peculiarities shared by the two parts of *Solomon and Saturn* could suggest that they were composed by the same poet.

Since the test of the auxiliary and verbal is only one of the linguistic criteria in establishing authorship, further support in the form of lexical, stylistic, and literary evidence should be amassed. It would also be interesting to pursue the problem of authorship in other Old English verse texts, such as *Guthlac*, the second part of which might be attributable to Cynewulf while the first is more probably non-Cynewulfian.[12]

7.3 Verse and Prose

According to McIntosh, the following five stylistic genres are discernible in Old English literature:[13]

1 Classical verse
2 Late debased verse
3 Ælfric's style in his *Lives of Saints*
4 Wulfstan's style
5 Ordinary prose

The classical verse category refers to those poems that, for the most part, obey the rules of Sievers whereas the late 'debased' verse shows various metrical anomalies proscribed in the classical poetry. In late verse, for instance, half-lines are occasionally connected by rhyme and alliteration or by rhyme alone; alliteration falls on the second lift of the off-verse; half-lines often fail to conform to Sievers's rhythmic types; and the use of Types D and E is in decline. Late poems like the *Paris Psalter* make relatively little use of traditional poetic diction, with few poetic compounds, kennings, or formulae.

12 Krapp-Dobbie (*Anglo-Saxon Poetic Records*, 3: xxxiif.).
13 McIntosh (1949).

EXERCISE: Metrical Anomalies in the Late Poetry

Read the following passage from a *Chronicle* poem, the *Death of Alfred* (labelled as a debased poem by McIntosh), which describes the murder of Prince Alfred, son of Æthelred, at the hands of Earl Godwine in the year 1036. List metrical anomalies that would not occur in a classical poem like *Beowulf*:

Ac Godwine hine þā gelette and hine on hæft sette,
and his gefēran hē tōdrāf, and sume mislīce ofslōh;
sume hī man wið fēo sealde, sume hrēowlīce ācwealde,
sume hī man bende, sume hī man blende,
sume hamelode, sume hættode.
Ne wearð drēorlīcre dǣd gedōn on þison earde,
syþþan Dene cōmon and hēr frið namon. (*DAlf* 6–12)

[But then Godwine prevented him, and put him in captivity, and he dispersed his followers, and killed some in various ways; some of them were sold for money, some cruelly killed, some of them were fettered, some of them were blinded, some hamstringed, some scalped. No crueller deed was done in this country after the Danes came, and made peace here.]

Ælfric's style is known as rhythmical prose, which shares both alliteration and long-line structure with the poetry. In the following passage on the death of St Oswald, each 'on-verse' is linked with the 'off-verse' by alliteration:[14]

Æfter ðan ðe **A**ugustīnus tō **E**ngla lande becōm
wæs sum **æ**ðel(e) cyning, **Ō**swold gehāten,
on Norðhymbra **l**ande, ge**l**ȳfed swȳþe on God. (*Oswald* 1–3)

[After Augustine came to England, there was a noble king called Oswald in the land of Northumbria, having much faith in God.]

14 Cited from Cassidy and Ringler (1971). In manuscripts of *Lives of Saints* and other alliterative works by Ælfric, the line and half-line divisions are often marked with points or other punctuation.

Ælfric's rhythmical prose, however, differs from the poetry in that unstressed syllables occur more freely, making his half-line longer than the classical half-line. In *Beowulf*, as mentioned in 5.1, the average length of a half-line is slightly less than 5 syllables, which is also the case with the late *Maldon*. In rhythmical prose, on the other hand, a 'half-line' consists of 7 syllables on average. This also explains Ælfric's preference for half-lines beginning with a preposition to yield an extra unstressed syllable, as in *mid lӯtlum werode* 'with a small troop' (*Oswald* 15a), *mid welwillend(um) mōde* 'with benevolent mind' (*Oswald* 59b), *mid blīþum mōde* 'with blithe mind' (*Oswald* 66b), and the like. In verse, inflectional forms often occur instead of prepositional phrases, as in *lӯtle werede* (*GenA* 2093b), *blīðe mōde* (*PPs* 89.18.3b). See 6.3 above.

Like late 'debased' verse, Ælfric's rhythmical prose allows alliterative anomalies, such as an alliterating second lift in the off-verse, alliterative precedence of second compound elements to first ones, and alliteration between the consonant clusters *sc-/sp-/st-* and the single consonant *s-*, represented respectively in the three instances below:

/ / /
Nū hæfð hē þone **w**urðmynt on þǣre ēcan **w**orulde (*Oswald* 277)
[Now he has honour in the eternal world]

/ / / /
Sende ðā tō Scot**l**ande, þǣr se ge**l**ēafa wæs ðā (*Oswald* 48)
[(He) then sent to Scotland, where (there) was the faith then]

/ / / /
embe his **s**āwle þearfa oððe his **Sc**yppendes beboda (*Oswald* 244)
[(he hardly thought) about the needs of his soul or his Creator's commands]

In addition to these non-classical features, Ælfric's rhythmical prose contains few poetic compounds, kennings, or formulae.

Wulfstan's rhythmical prose employs a two-stress-phrase structure resembling the rhythm of the classical half-line. To illustrate Wulfstan's rhythmic pattern, a passage from the *Sermo Lupi ad Anglos* is conveniently divided into two-stress-phrase units:[15]

15 The lineation follows McIntosh (1949: 131).

/ /
Ne dohte hit nū lange
/ /
inne ne **ū**te
/ /
ac wæs **h**ere and **h**unger
/ /
bryne and **b**lōdgyte
/ /
on gewelhwylcan ende
/ /
oft and gelōme
/ /
and ūs st**alu** and cw**alu**
/ /
strīc and **st**eorfa
/ /
orfcwealm and **u**ncoðu
/ /
hōl and **h**ete
/ /
and **r**ȳpera **r**ēaflāc
/ /
derede swīðe þearle (*WHom* 20.1 50–3, arranged into two-stress phrase-units)

[Nothing has prospered now for a long time here or elsewhere but (there) has been war and famine, burning and bloodshed in every region often and again; and stealing and killing, plague and pestilence, cattle-plague and disease, slander and hostility, and plunder by robbers have damaged us very severely]

The two-stress phrases are often linked by alliteration (e.g., lines 2, 3, 4, 8, 9, 10, 11) and occasionally by rhyme (e.g., line 7). Alliteration does not, however, normally extend beyond the two-stress phrases to form a long line. Finally, ordinary prose includes Alfredian prose, most of the *Chronicle*, and most of Ælfric's *Catholic Homilies*, where both alliterative and rhythmic systems are lacking.

The first two genres (i.e., classical verse and late debased verse) are generally regarded as verse appropriate for inclusion in the *Anglo-Saxon Poetic Records*. However, as already noted, Ælfric's rhythmical prose shares important features with poetry, such as a long-line structure with two half-lines linked by alliteration. In particular, as we have seen above, there are quite a few resemblances between Ælfric's rhythmical prose and late 'debased' verse. Sometimes, Ælfric was even more conservative in his 'versification' than late Old English poets; while the poet of the *Death of Alfred* (see EXERCISE 'Metrical Anomalies in the Late Poetry' above) used rhyme as well as alliteration, Ælfric generally avoided using rhyme to link half-lines. This has led some scholars to expand the boundary of Old English poetry so as to incorporate Ælfric's rhythmical prose.[16]

Drawing the line between poetry and prose is not only a matter of including or excluding 'verselike' prose but also of reexamining the 'authorized' poetic corpus. We have tacitly assumed that the verse texts included in the *Anglo-Saxon Poetic Records* (hereafter abbreviated as *ASPR*) define the poetic corpus. This is, however, not the case. The *Death of Alfred*, a *Chronicle* poem with striking metrical anomalies, is included in the *ASPR* not because of its metrical form but simply 'following the practice of earlier editors.'[17] In addition to the six poems printed in the *ASPR*, other passages in the *Chronicles* are often identified as poetry.[18] In particular, the variant version of the *Death of Edgar* in MS Cotton Tiberius B. iv (D) and MS Laud Misc. 636 (E), although excluded from the *ASPR*, has often been regarded as verse:[19]

× /   × × /   /   × / ×
Hēr **Ea**dgar gefōr,   **A**ngla reccend,
/   \ × ×   /   ×   /   ×   /   \ ×
Westseaxena **w**ine,   and **M**yrcna **m**undbora.
/   ×   ×   / ×   ×   /   / ×
Cūð wæs þæt wīde   geond feola þēoda,

16 Clemoes (1966), Kuhn (1973), and Bredehoft (2004a, 2005a), among others. With reference to metrico-syntactic irregularities, other scholars differentiate Ælfric's rhythmical works from Old English poetry including the debased poems (see, for instance, Russom (1987), Momma (1997), and Mitchell (2005)).

17 Krapp-Dobbie (*Anglo-Saxon Poetic Records*, 6: v).

18 Seventeen verse passages (including six poems in the *ASPR*) are recognized by Plummer (1892–9) whereas Swanton (2000) distinguishes ten poetic passages.

19 McIntosh (1949) includes this poem under his late debased poetry. Robinson and Stanley's facsimile volume of miscellaneous Old English poems includes this poem as well as another *Chronicle* poem known as *William the Conqueror* (cf. Robinson and Stanley 1991). The variant version of the *Death of Edgar* is cited with slight modifications from the D manuscript edited by Cubbin (1996).

x / x / \ x x x / x /
þæt afaren **Ead**mundes ofer ga[n]e[t]es beð
/ x x x / x / x x / x
cynegas hyne **wīde** **wurðodon** swīðe,
x x x x / x x x x x / x
bugon tō þām **c**yninge swā him wæs ge**c**ynde.
x x / x / x x / x /
Næs <se> flota swā r**ang** ne se here swā str**ang**
x x / x / x / x x / x
þæt on **A**ngelcynne **ǣ**s him gefætte,
x xx x x / x / / \ x/ x
þā hwīle þe se æþela **c**yning **c**ynestōl gerehte

(*The Death of Edgar*, variant version)

[In this year Edgar passed away, ruler of the English, friend of the West-Saxons, and protector of the Mercians. That was widely known throughout many nations, so that kings widely and greatly honoured the son of Edmund over the gannet's bath (and) bowed to the king as was proper to him. No fleet was proud, no army strong enough to fetch booty for itself in England while the noble king held the throne]

This poem does not seem to be metrically 'inferior' to late poems in the *ASPR*. Metrically, most of the half-lines fit into Sievers's basic types, Type A verses being the most common (e.g., 1b, 3a, 5a, 5b, 8a, 8b). There are no verses with less than three syllables or with a verse-final dip of more than one syllable. Half-lines are linked by alliteration, though there are some anomalous lines: in the on- and off-verse of line 2 alliteration occurs within the half-lines but not across; in 5a, only the second lift participates in alliteration whereas in 6b with the first lift suppressed the 'second' lift alliterates. Metrical irregularities of these sorts do occur in late poetry, however. Furthermore, as rhyme links the half-lines only once (between *rang* and *strang* in line 7), the poet of the *Death of Edgar* (variant version) seems to be more sparing in the use of rhyme than the poet of the *Death of Alfred*. The prosaic phrase *þā hwīle þe* occurs in the last line of this work, but the same phrase is attested in *Maldon* (see 5.1).

Although the present book has dealt primarily with metrical practices in so-called classical Old English poetry, the late literary works (whether they are labelled verse or prose) show relaxation of the metrical rules to such different degrees that it would hardly be possible to find criteria that distinguish some as poetry and others as prose. Instead, the metrical rules we have studied can help to measure 'distance' (a better term than 'deviation') from the 'classical' tradition.

References and Suggestions for Further Reading

Metre and Dating: Amos (1980) examines the validity of various linguistic tests for determining the date of poetry, concluding that '[o]f the chronological tests for dating Old English poetry discussed in this monograph, very few have the reliability associated with the great *Lautgesetze*' (167). Chase (1981) is a collection of important papers discussing the date of *Beowulf* from multiple viewpoints without reaching a consensus. On papers in the collection more or less related to metre, see Cable (1981), Pope (1981), and Stanley (1981). More recently, Liuzza (1995) questions the use of metrical evidence for dating, stating that '[i]f poems were composed lexically rather than metrically—by improvising on the common stock of traditional collocations, remembered expressions, and accepted formulae with only secondary attention to the rules discerned by modern descriptive metre—then any notion of dating based on these patterns must be questionable' (287).

Fulk (1989, 1992, 2007b) goes against the stream by attempting to set a fairly reliable terminus ad quem for *Beowulf*, which adhered relatively well to Kaluza's Law in a strict sense (see 4.2.4). '*Beowulf* would then seem to have been composed,' he concludes, 'at a time when these etymologically short endings were still distinctly differentiated from long ones, and that would imply a date of composition no later than about AD 725 if the poem is not Northumbrian in origin, otherwise no later than about AD 825' (Fulk 2007b: 319). Fulk's theory has been supported by Clemoes (1995) on cultural evidence, by Lapidge (2000) on palaeographic evidence, and Cronan (2004) on lexical evidence. For those scholars who challenge Fulk's view, see Hutcheson (2004) and Frank (2007), among others. Fulk (2007b) responds to Hutcheson's criticism.

For dating of the other Old English poetry (especially the Cynewulf canon), see Conner (2001) and Fulk (2001).

Metre and Authorship: On the use of Kuhn's Second Law for determining the Cynewulf canon, see Momma (1997: 73, 188). In his conclusion, Donoghue (1987b: 104–16) discusses the problem of authorship with reference to *Solomon and Saturn* and the Cynewulf signed poems. By examining the use of contracted and uncontracted negative forms in the signed poems, Terasawa (2005) supports Donoghue's view that *Christ B* and the *Fates of the Apostles* might not be attributable to Cynewulf. Fulk

(2001: 9), on the other hand, argues for the homogeneity of the four poems bearing Cynewulf's runic signatures.

Verse and Prose: For the five genres in Old English literature, see McIntosh (1949). On the basis of nine metrical criteria, Grinda (1984) classifies verse texts according to the scale of metrical/stylistic strictness, ranging from *Beowulf* and *Exodus* at the top to the *Meters of Boethius,* the *Paris Psalter, Christ and Satan*, or the *Battle of Maldon* at the bottom.

The question as to whether Ælfric's alliterative-rhythmical works are verse or prose has provoked much controversy. Pope regards them rather as 'a mildly ornamental, rhythmically ordered prose than as a debased, pedestrian poetry' (1967–8, I: 105). Mitchell states that 'Ælfric's alliterative prose, though or because it lacks the alliteration and rhythm of poetry, is good prose' (2005: 359). Russom (1987: 133–44) observes minute metrical differences between *Beowulf* and Ælfric's homily on St Oswald, the latter of which provides no example of a half-line structure common in *Beowulf*, i.e., a Type A verse consisting of two trochaic words. Momma (1997) argues that her syntactic rules (her revised version of Kuhn's Laws) could objectively differentiate between verse included in the *ASPR* and Ælfric's rhythmical prose, the former of which observes the rules but not the latter (although she does not demonstrate that Ælfric's rhythmical works neglect the laws). See also Fulk (2004).

On the other hand, some scholars expand the boundary of Old English poetry so as to incorporate Ælfric's rhythmical prose. See also Kuhn (1973) and Bredehoft (2004a).

On the basis of lexical as well as metrical evidence, Stanley (1985) identifies verse passages in the prose homily from Corpus Christi College Cambridge, MS 201, to which he gives the title 'the Judgement of the Damned.' Scragg (1992), however, regards the passages not as 'a poem incorporated into the homily' but rather as 'a feature of the homilist's own style' (51).

Bredehoft (2004b) shows that 'irregular' poems (including those excluded from the *ASPR*) are often differentiated in manuscript from surrounding prose in terms of punctuation, spacing, and capitalization, providing 'a broader, more inclusive canon of Old English verse than that of the *ASPR*' (143).

Appendix A Suggested Answers to the Exercises

Chapter 1

EXERCISE: Alliterative Patterns

Examples 2 and 4 show acceptable patterns of alliteration whereas examples 1 (only the second lift alliterating in the on-verse), 3 (only the second lift alliterating in the off-verse), and 5 (double alliteration in the off-verse) are metrically anomalous.

EXERCISE: The Four-syllable Principle and Word-choice

With the shorter *gēn*, the half-line would result in a verse of three syllables, which is too short: **fremmað gēn*. For further discussions of choice between morphological variants, see 5.2.1.

Chapter 2

EXERCISE: Consonantal and Vocalic Alliteration

Alliterating letters are in bold:

1) **ġ**eongum **g**ārwigan   **ġ**ēoce gefremman
2) **c**ūþe næssas;   **ċ**ēol up geþrang
3) **st**ōd on **st**apole,   geseah **st**ēapne hrōf
4) **i**dese tō **e**fnanne,   þēah ðe hīo **ǣ**nlīcu sȳ
5) Ā**r**īs, **r**īces weard,   uton h**r**aðe fēran

EXERCISE: To Emend or Not to Emend

Although substitution of synonymous *ābrēat* 'killed' for *ofslōh* has been proposed (cf. Holthausen 1905: 114), most scholars have chosen to follow the manuscript reading without accepting such a drastic conjecture.

EXERCISE: Breaches of the Alliterative Rules

1) Violating the Alliterative Rule of Precedence
2) Only the second lift alliterating in the off-verse / Violating the Alliterative Rule of Precedence
3) Only the second lift alliterating in the off-verse (note that the past participle *hāten* serves as the first lift)
4) Violating the principle of Left Dominance (note that the past participle, i.e., *tōbrocen* is of the same metrical importance as the noun, i.e., *scyldburh*)
5) Violating the principle of Left Dominance

Chapter 3

EXERCISE: Identifying Rhythmic Stress

/ / / /

1) **g**eongum ond ealdum swylc him **G**od sealde (note that *sealde*, the finite verb, is a particle displaced from clause-initial position and receives rhythmic stress)

/ / / /

2) sē þe his **w**ordes ge**w**eald **w**īde hæfde (note that *hæfde* receives rhythmic stress as a particle displaced from clause-initial position)

/ / / /

3) **ē**ce drihten, þæs þe hē **Ā**bel slōg (*slōg* receives rhythmic stress as a displaced particle)

/ / /

4) þā wæs æfter **w**iste **w**ōp up āhafen (note that the on-verse has only one rhythmic stress)

/ / / /

5) **m**ǣre þēoden **m**ondrēamum from (note that *from* receives rhythmic stress as a preposition (proclitic) displaced from its normal position before the noun)

EXERCISE: Patronymics

In *Beowulf*, trisyllabic names in the genitive like *Ecglāfes*, *Healfdenes*, and *Wīhstānes* form a half-line with monosyllabic *bearn*, *maga* (resolved), *mago* (resolved), and *sunu* (resolved): *Ecglāfes bearn* (499b), *mago Ecglāfes* (1465b), *sunu Ecglāfes* (1808a), *bearn Healfdenes* (469a), *maga Healfdenes* (189b, etc), *mago Healfdenes* (1867a, 2011b), *sunu Healfdenes* (268a, etc), *Healfdenes sunu* (1009b), *Wīhstānes sunu* (3076b), *sunu Wīhstānes* (3120b). Note that some metrically possible combinations (e.g., *maga Wīhstānes*, *Wīhstānes bearn*) are not attested, perhaps for non-metrical reasons. On the other hand, disyllabic names in the genitive like *Scyldes* and *Wælses* can be combined with disyllabic *eafera* (resolved), e.g., *Wælses eafera* (897a) and *Scyldes eafera* (19a), but not with monosyllabic *bearn*, *maga* (resolved), *mago* (resolved), and *sunu* (resolved).

EXERCISE: Identifying Rhythmic Types

Rhythmic types are given in round brackets after the half-lines:

x x /| /x x /|/x
Hwæt, wē Gār-Dena (C) in geārdagum, (C)

/ |/ \ x / x| / x
þēodcyninga (D1) þrym gefrūnon, (A1)

x x /|/ x / x | / x
hū ðā æþelingas (C) ellen fremedon. (A1)

x / | /x / x| / x
Oft Scyld Scēfing (C) sceaþena þrēatum, (A1)

/ x | / x / \ xx|/
monegum mǣgþum (A1) meodosetla ofteāh, (E)

/ x x|/ x x x /|x /
egsode eorlas, (A1) syððan ǣrest wearð (B)

/ \|/ x x x /|x x /
fēasceaft funden. (A2) Hē þæs frōfre gebād: (B)

/ x x| / x / \ x |/
wēox under wolcnum, (A1) weorðmyndum þāh, (E)

x x x |/ x xx|/ |/ \ x
oð þæt him ǣghwylc (A3) þāra ymbsittendra (D1 with anacrusis)

xx /|/x / x | / x
ofer hronrāde (C) hȳran scolde, (A1)

/ x| / x x x / |/x
gomban gyldan. (A1) Þæt wæs gōd cyning. (C)

Note: In verse 9b, *þāra* is often omitted since the off-verse (of Type D) normally forbids anacrusis. See, for instance, Klaeber (3rd ed., 1950) and Fulk, Bjork, and Niles (2008), the latter of which underdot and ignore *þāra*. The metrical classification of all the verses in *Beowulf* is made in Pope (1966), Bliss (1967, 1995), Kendall (1991), and Suzuki (1996a) according to their own systems. Vickman's scansion is based on Bliss's theory (cf. Vickman 1990).

EXERCISE: Hypermetric Verses

```
 / x x   x| / x | / x   x x   x  x | / x   x| / x
swǣtan on þā swīðran healfe.  Eall ic wæs mid sorgum gedrēfed,
 /  x  x  x  x x| / x  x|/ x   x x x  x | / x| / x
forht ic wæs for þǣre fægran gesyhðe.  Geseah ic þæt fūse bēacen
  / x | / x x | /x     xx  x  x  x| / x  x| / x
wendan wǣdum ond blēom;  hwīlum hit wæs mid wǣtan bestēmed,
 x| /  x | / x | / x    xx  x |/ x x| / x
beswȳled mid swātes gange,  hwīlum mid since gegyrwed.
```

Chapter 4

EXERCISE: Half-lines of Three or Fewer Syllables

Listed below are the readings of verses 1404b, 2139a, and 2488a in the major editions of *Beowulf* published after 1950. 'MS.' indicates that the editions retain the manuscript readings:

	Klaeber (1950)	*ASPR*, vol. 4 (1953)	Heyne-von Schaubert (1963)	Magoun (1966)	Nickel (1976–82)
gegnum fōr (1404b)	[swā] gegnum fōr	[þǣr hēo] gegnum fōr	MS.	[swā] gegnum fōr	MS.
in ðām sele (2139a)	in ðām [gūð]sele	in ðām [gūð]sele	in ðām [gūð]sele	on þǣm [gūþ]sele	in ðām [gūð]sele
hrēas blāc (2488a)	hrēas [heoro]blāc	hrēas [hilde]blāc	hrēas [hilde]blāc	hrǣ[w]blāc [gehrēas]	hrēas [heoro]blāc

	Chickering (1977)	Crépin (1991)	Jack (1994)	Wrenn-Bolton (1996)	Swanton (1997)
gegnum fōr (1404b)	MS.	MS.	[swā] gegnum fōr	MS.	[þǣr hēo] gegnum fōr
in ðām sele (2139a)	in ðām [gūð]sele	MS.	in ðām [gūð]sele	in ðām [gūð]sele	in ðām [gūð]sele
hrēas blāc (2488a)	hrēas [heoro]blāc	MS.	hrēas [hilde]blāc	hrēas [heoro]blāc	hrēas [heoro]blāc

	Trask (1997)	Alexander (2000)	Slade (2002–3)	Kiernan (2004)	Mitchell-Robinson (2006)
gegnum fōr (1404b)	gegnum f[e]r[de]	MS.	MS.	MS.	[þǣr] gegnum fōr
in ðām sele (2139a)	in ðām [gūð]sele	in ðām [gūð]sele	in ðām [grund]sele	in ðām [grund]s(ele)	in ðām [grund]sele
hrēas blāc (2488a)	hrēas [hilde] blāc	hrēas [heoro]blāc	hrēas [heaþo]blāc	hrēas [heaþo]blāc	hrēas [heoro]blāc

	Fulk, Bjork, & Niles (2008)
gegnum fōr (1404b)	[þǣr] gegnum fōr
in ðām sele (2139a)	in ðām [gūð]sele
hrēas blāc (2488a)	hrēas [hilde]blāc

EXERCISE: Contraction, Parasiting, and Syncopation

/ x /x
1) **m**an geþēon Type A1 (Expand the contracted *-þēon*.)

x x x / / x
2) cwæð þæt se ælmihtịga Type C (Ignore the syncopatable vowel in *ælmihtiga*.)

/ x / x
3) **ō**þres dōgọres Type A1 (Ignore the syncopatable vowel in *dōgores*.)

/ \ x /
4) **w**ælfāgne **w**intẹr Type E (Assume the nonparasiting form in *winter*.)

/ \ /x
5) **m**orþọrbed strēd Type A2 (Assume the nonparasiting form in *morþor-* and expand the contracted form *strēd*.)

Chapter 5

EXERCISE: *Þendan* vs. *Þā hwīle (þe)*

The marginal gloss would suggest that the corrector himself was not familiar with the archaic *ðenden* or might have thought the audience would not recognize it. Note that *ðenden* occurs only seven times in prose (against some seventy-five times in verse). See Mitchell (1969: 71; 1985: §§ 2629, 2634–5).

EXERCISE: *Gīeta* vs. *Gīet*

In example 2, the use of the monosyllabic *gīet* would produce an unmetrical verse of only three syllables (**næs þā gīet*) whereas in the other half-lines the replacement of the disyllabic form by the monosyllabic would result in unscannable verses (**sumne þā gēt*, **āwēr þā gēt*, **Wē sculon ðēah gīt*, **ðēah ðū hī nū gēt*). It is interesting to note here that in each of the passages of the *Prose Boethius* corresponding to the *Meters* (except example 1) monosyllabic forms occur instead of disyllabic variants (cf. *Bo* 33.25 *gīt*; *Bo* 34.3 *gēt*; *Bo* 101.22 *gēt*; *Bo* 105.21 *gēot*). Except for two instances (cf. *GenA* 155b, *Dream* 28b), the other verse instances of *gīeta* are also found in metrical contexts where the shorter form would be unacceptable (cf. *GenA* 116b,[1] 993b, 1453a, 1635b, 2468b; *Brun* 66b).

EXERCISE: Harpers in Old English Literature

The *Beowulf* poet often refers to the music of a harp but never mentions its player. The word *hearpere* 'harper' is not only absent from *Beowulf* but also from other verse texts, with the exception of *Psalm 50* 4, where this derivative is used for David. Old English prose writers show no hesitation about using *hearpere* and provide twenty-four instances. In the *Prose Boethius*, each of seven occurrences of *hearpere* is used for Orpheus, the great mythical musician. Since the story of Orpheus is left out in the *Meters of Boethius*, we cannot tell whether the versifier would have used this word for this legendary harper.

EXERCISE: Restoring *Beowulf* 3153a

Klaeber (3rd ed., 1950) restores *hearm-dagas* 'evil-days,' but this reading does not account for a letter *g* preceding *gas* with an intervening space, which Kiernan (2004) claims to see in the manuscript. This emendation is adopted by Trask (1997). Klaeber also suggests that the reading *hefige dagas* 'grievous days' is possible (1950: 459). Nickel (1976–82), Crépin (1991), Jack (1994), Wrenn-Bolton (1996), and Fulk, Bjork, and Niles (2008) follow Mackie (1941) and adopt *here-geongas* or *here-gangas* 'invasions.' Krapp-Dobbie (*Anglo-Saxon Poetic Records*, vol. 4), Swanton (1997), and Mitchell-Robinson (2006) read *hēofung-dagas* 'mourning-days,' which is proposed by Pope in his first edition of *The Rhythm of* Beowulf (1942). (In his revised edition, however, Pope supports Mackie's

1 In the manuscript, *þa gyta* is corrected to *þa gyt*.

conjecture instead of his own reading.) In the light of compound constraints, the restoration *hēofung-dagas* would be less likely because it results in the unacceptable pattern of **hilde-fruma*. There is no way to avoid this metrically anomalous pattern by reference to parasiting or syncopation. Both *here-geongas* and *hearm-dagas* are metrically acceptable. The syntactic phrase *hefige dagas* is not subject to the compound constraint. *Here-geongas* would be tenable because it 'better fits the physical requirements and is superior in meaning to any of the conjectured compounds with *dagas*' (Pope 1967: xxvf.). For fuller discussion, see Terasawa (1994: 20).

EXERCISE: Poetic Compounds for the Drinking Hall

To denote 'mead/wine-hall,' the Old English poetic corpus provides the following instances: *medo-ærn*, *medo-heal(l)*, *medu-seld*, *wīn-ærn*, *wīn-reced*, *wīn-sæl*, and *wīn-sele*. Except for *wīn-sæl*, all these compounds are found in *Beowulf*. The two compounds *medo-ærn* and *medu-seld* are peculiar to the epic. It is important to note that the second elements of the resolvable sequence (*-reced* and *-sele*) occur exclusively with *wīn-*, while those of the non-resolvable sequence (*-ærn*, *-heal(l)*, *-seld*) form compounds with *medo-* as well as with *wīn-*. The absence of **medo-reced* and **medo-sele* is due to the constraint on the sequence of the *here-toga* pattern.

EXERCISE: *Helle* Sequence

It is important to note that alliteration does not fall on the first element of *helle fȳr* but on the preceding adjective *grim* 'fierce,' which alliterates with *gearo* 'ready.' In Old English poetry, it is extremely rare for the first element of a compound to fail to alliterate. When *gūð* 'battle,' one of the most productive first elements, forms compounds, for instance, it invariably alliterates on the sound /g/ except for *Gūþlāf* (*Finn* 16). Thus, the alliterative pattern in *Christ C* 1269 points to the syntactic analysis of *helle fȳr*.

Chapter 6

EXERCISE: Uninflected Past Participle

The past participle *forgrunden* is uninflected probably because the inflected form *forgrundenne* would result in an unmetrical verse: no Type A half-line is allowed to end with two unstressed syllables: **wúnduͯn foͯrgrúndeͯnneͯ*. Nor is the Type D*1 analysis with a secondary stress on the second syllable of *-grundenne* plausible because Type D verses are rarely expanded by a disyllabic dip immediately after the first lift (see Campbell 1938: 19).

EXERCISE: Weak Adjectives without a Demonstrative

When weak adjectives follow nouns, the demonstrative occurs either before or after nouns in *Beowulf*, as in *ac se maga geonga* 'but the young kinsman' (2675a) and *in sele þām hēan* 'in the high hall' (713b). The insertion of a demonstrative after the noun would result in a half-line of unknown type: *_bēahsele se beorhta_. If the demonstrative was inserted before the noun, the verse would be of Type A2 with anacrusis. But in verse 1177a with *-sele* resolved, the first syntactic group (i.e., *bēahsele*) is of the same metrical length as the second (i.e., *beorhta*). Under this circumstance, as mentioned in 3.4, anacrusis is quite rare: *_se bēahsele beorhta_.

EXERCISE: Multiple Negation

As the line lacks alliteration, *nǣnigum* is to be emended to *ǣnigum* to provide vocalic alliteration. This emendation has been adopted by most editors although Swanton retains the original reading because 'lack of alliteration in a second half-line is by no means uncommon in VB verse' (1996: 121). The conjecture is syntactically sound in consideration of the reluctance to multiply negatives in poetry.

EXERCISE: Is *Se* a Demonstrative or a Relative Pronoun?

Krapp-Dobbie (*Anglo-Saxon Poetic Records*, vol. 4), Jack (1994), Mitchell-Robinson (2006), and Fulk, Bjork, and Niles (2008) put a semi-colon after *ȳðgewinne*, taking *se* as a demonstrative pronoun ('it was within full of ornaments and gold filigrees') while Wyatt-Chambers (1920) and Wrenn-Bolton (1996) place a comma after verse 2412a, taking *se* as a relative pronoun. Swanton (1997) follows the latter with the translation 'which within was full of decorated objects and filigree.'

EXERCISE: Kuhn's Laws and Textual Criticism

The addition of *selfa* between two particles results in the violation of Kuhn's First Law. (If displaced, the auxiliary *mōst* would receive rhythmic stress, which would result in an unattested verse type.) As Donoghue suggests concerning the position of *selfa*, '[p]lacing it after *mōst* would eliminate the violation and preserve the alliteration and sense of Krapp's emendation' (1987b: 15). The verse *ac þū mōst [selfa] heonon* belongs to Type B.

EXERCISE: Kuhn's Laws and Punctuation

As it begins with a preposition, verse 1913b cannot be clause-initial. According to Kendall (1991: 40), if *lyftgeswenced* is taken as 'wind-battered' and linked to the following verse (with the comma shifted after *geþrang*), verse 1913b ceases to be clause-initial and there is no violation of Kuhn's Second Law:

> cēol up geþrang,
> lyftgeswenced on lande stōd.
> [The ship drove up (ashore); wind-battered, (it) rested on land]

This reading and punctuation have been adopted in Jack (1994) and Fulk, Bjork, and Niles (2008). Bosworth-Toller also gloss *lyftgeswenced* as 'weather-beaten.'

Chapter 7

EXERCISE: The 'G' Test for Dating

Velar and palatal *g* alliterate in lines 2 (*ġifena*, *ġinnan*, *grunde*, and *ġear-we*), 22 (*goldwine*, *gumena*, and *ġytesālum*), 9 (*ġirwan* and *gumena*), 238 (*onġēaton* and *grame*), and 279 (*gold-*, *-ġifan*, *gæstes*, and *ġēsne*.). Griffith (1997: 26, n. 90) does not approve the alliteration of different g's in lines 22 and 279. In line 149, however, the alliteration of two different g's results in an anomalous metrical pattern where the second lift of the off-verse (occupied by *gān*) alliterates with *ġinnan* and *tōġēanes*. It follows that the poet made velar and palatal *g* alliterating but 'was reluctant to use this phonetic license freely' (Griffith 1997: 26). If late Old English poets were able to follow traditional metrical practice, the choice between the traditional and later alliterative pattern would be a matter of personal poetic style. The fact that a verse text exhibits alliteration between two different *g*'s does not necessarily indicate that it was composed early, but it might be safe to assign a late composition date to verse texts that consistently avoid alliterating velar *g* with palatal *g*.

EXERCISE: Cynewulf's Signed Poems

A single author might change his/her style during his/her writing career. Cynewulf might have composed the signed poems at significantly different stages, which might account for the linguistic discrepancies. On the other hand, an author might imitate his/her predecessor's style. Hence linguistic and stylistic similarities do not necessarily point to single authorship.

EXERCISE: Metrical Anomalies in the Late Poetry

Listed below are metrical anomalies in the *Death of Alfred*:

Use of rhyme instead of alliteration to link the half-lines (ll. 6, 8). Probably imperfect rhyme in lines 7 (between *(tōdr)āf* and *(ofsl)ōh*) and 12 (between *(c)ōmon* and *(n)amon*).

Use of both rhyme and alliteration to link the half-lines (ll. 9, 10). Note that line 11 is the only instance where alliteration alone links the half-lines.

Anacrusis in the off-verse (8b, 11b)

Anacrusis before Type E (11a)

Appendix B Some Tips for Scanning Half-lines, with Sample Scansions

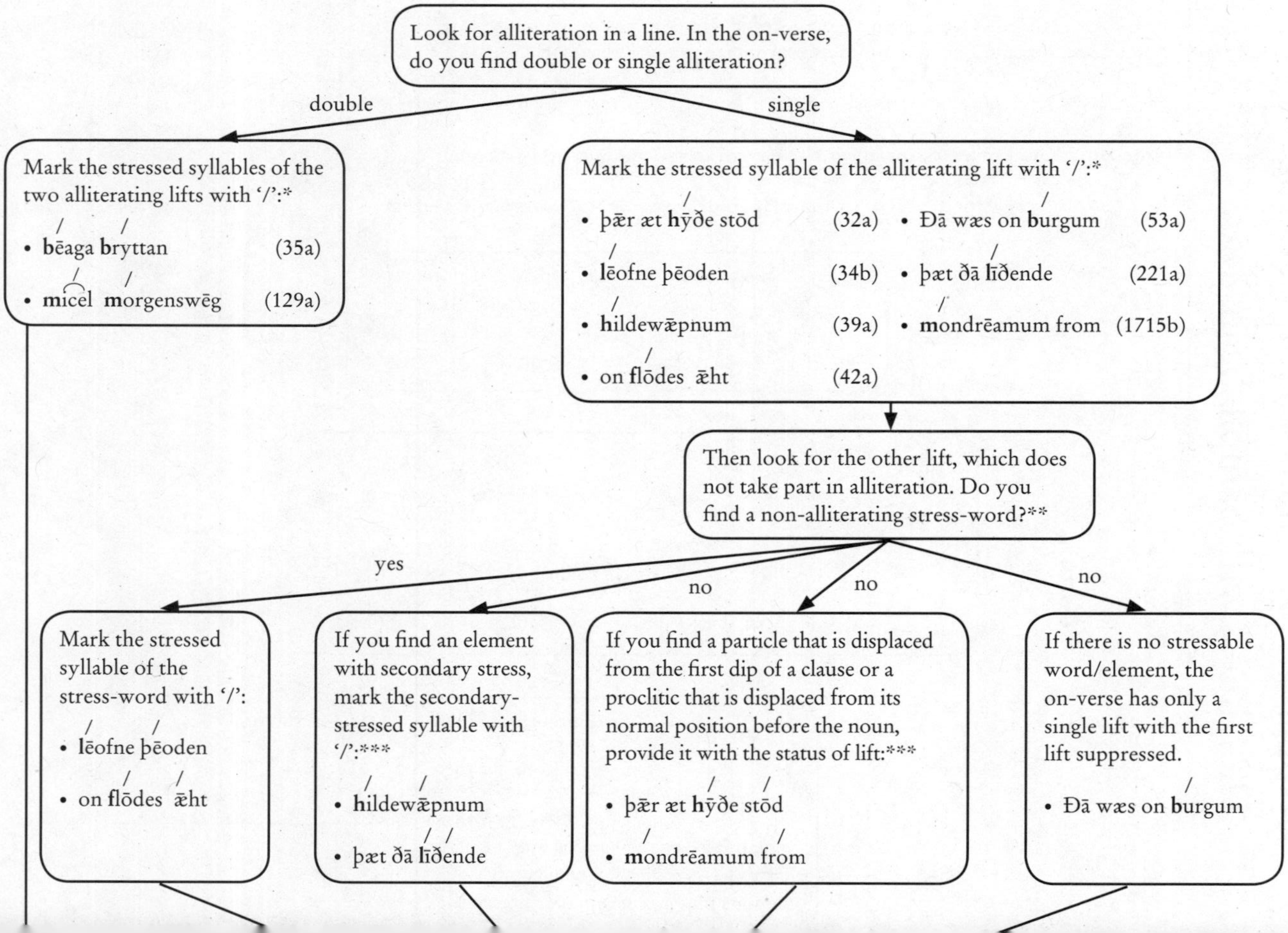
Look for alliteration in a line. In the on-verse, do you find double or single alliteration?
double
single
Mark the stressed syllables of the two alliterating lifts with '/':*
• bēaga bryttan (35a)
• micel morgenswēg (129a)
Mark the stressed syllable of the alliterating lift with '/':*
• þǣr æt hȳðe stōd (32a)
• lēofne þēoden (34b)
• hildewǣpnum (39a)
• on flōdes ǣht (42a)
• Ðā wæs on burgum (53a)
• þæt ðā līðende (221a)
• mondrēamum from (1715b)
Then look for the other lift, which does not take part in alliteration. Do you find a non-alliterating stress-word?**
yes
no
no
no
Mark the stressed syllable of the stress-word with '/':
• lēofne þēoden
• on flōdes ǣht
If you find an element with secondary stress, mark the secondary-stressed syllable with '/':***
• hildewǣpnum
• þæt ðā līðende
If you find a particle that is displaced from the first dip of a clause or a proclitic that is displaced from its normal position before the noun, provide it with the status of lift:***
• þǣr æt hȳðe stōd
• mondrēamum from
If there is no stressable word/element, the on-verse has only a single lift with the first lift suppressed.
• Ðā wæs on burgum

Besides the two lifts, if you find another stressable element (e.g. a stress-word, an element with secondary stress), provide it with the status of half-lift '\':

```
 /    /       \
• micel  morgenswēg
  /    \       /
• mondrēamum from
```

↓

Mark all the rest of the (unstressed) syllables with 'x'.

```
  x  x  / x  /         /  x  /  x            /    /  x  \
• þǣr æt hȳðe stōd   • hildewǣpnum       • micel  morgenswēg
  /   x  /  x          x   / x  /          x  x / /  x
• lēofne þēoden      • on flōdes  ǣht    • þæt ðā līðende
   /  x   /  x           x  x  x   /  x      /    \  x    /
• bēaga bryttan      • Ðā wæs on burgum  • mondrēamum from
```

↓

Look for (single) alliteration in the off-verse. Mark the stressed syllable of the alliterating lift with '/'. Then look for the other lift, which does not take part in alliteration, as you do for the on-verse above.

Hypermetric verses are excluded. Each of the examples above, which is cited from *Beowulf*, is referred to the book.

* Lift falls on a long syllable or two resolved syllables.

** Stress-words include nouns, adjectives, non-finite verbs (i.e. infinitives and participles), many adverbs, and heavy pronouns like *gehwylc* and *gehwæþer*.

*** Elements with secondary stress include second compound elements, certain suffixes such as *-ende*, *-en*, *-ra/-est*, *-ig*, *-ing*, *-lice*, *-nes*, *-sum*, and the (historically long) penultimate syllable of Class II weak verbs.

****Particles include finite verbs, demonstrative adverbs, personal pronouns, demonstrative pronouns, and some conjunctions. Proclitics include prepositions, demonstratives, possessives, copulative conjunctions, and prefixes. Undislocated particles and proclitics may sometimes bear rhythmic stress for emphasis.

Appendix C Glossary of Metrical Terms

Alliteration: A repetition of the same sound at the beginning of two or more stressed words in a line. The initial consonant clusters *sc-*, *sp-*, and *st-* may alliterate only with themselves. In classical poetry, palatal *g* and *c* alliterate with velar *g* and *c* respectively. Vocalic alliteration can take place between different vowels/diphthongs. See chapter 2.1.

Alliterative Rule of Precedence: A nominal (including an adjective, a participle, an infinitive, as well as a noun) normally takes precedence in alliteration over a finite verb. See 2.3.

Anacrusis: One or two extrametrical unstressed syllables that occasionally appear before the initial lift in verses of Types A and D. See 3.4.

A-verse: See **On-verse**.

B-verse: See **Off-verse**.

Caesura: a pause between the on-verse and the off-verse, usually indicated by spacing in edited texts.

Contraction/contracted: After the loss of intervocalic *h* or *w*, originally disyllabic words like *hēahan* undergo contraction to become monosyllabic, i.e., *hēan*. In Old English poetry, earlier uncontracted (disyllabic) forms are often assumed for the sake of metre. See 4.2.1.

Crossed alliteration: An ornate alliterative pattern where all four lifts in a line participate in alliteration in the pattern [AB: AB]. See 2.2.2.

Dip: A rhythmically unstressed part (marked with a cross '×' or crosses '××', '×××', etc.), comprising one or more unstressed syllables. See **Lift**.

Double alliteration: Occurrence of two alliterating lifts in a half-line. Double alliteration is allowed only in the on-verse.

Epenthetic: See **Parasiting/parasitic/parasite**.

First half-line: See **On-verse**.

Foot: A metrical unit smaller than a half-line but larger than a syllable. A foot usually consists of two metrical positions, i.e., the lift and the dip. See 3.2.2.

Four-syllable Principle: A rudimentary requirement that each half-line must satisfy. As each of the four metrical positions in a half-line is occupied by at least one (stressed or unstressed) syllable, a normal half-line must consist of four syllables at a minimum. See 4.1.

Half-lift: A half-lift is a syllable bearing a rhythmic stress that is subordinate to two other lifts in a half-line. A half-lift (marked with a backward stroke '\') most often falls on the root syllable of the second compound element but sometimes on the derivative syllable of certain suffixes.

Heavy verse: A verse with two lifts and a half-lift. See **Light verse** and **Normal verse.**

Hypermetric verse: A verse containing more than two feet and four metrical positions. Most hypermetric verses occur in sequence. See 3.5.

Kaluza's Law: According to Kaluza, the application of resolution depends on the metrical structure of the resolvable sequence. If a resolvable sequence ends with a long unstressed syllable, resolution does not take place. On the other hand, if the second syllable of the resolved sequence is short, resolution takes place. The law is generally inapplicable outside *Beowulf*. See 4.2.4.

Kuhn's Laws: Kuhn formulates two rules concerning the placement of particles and proclitics in a verse clause. His first law states that particles must be placed together in the first dip of a clause while his second law states that at the beginning of a clause, the dip must contain particles. Although Kuhn's First Law is generally observed, the second law admits quite a few exceptions. See 6.5.2.

Left Dominance: If an on-verse contains two nominals, say a noun and an adjective, alliteration falls on both words or on the word at the left, but not on the word at the right alone. See 2.3.

Lift: A rhythmically stressed syllable in a line, which can participate in alliteration. A lift (marked with a stroke '/') normally requires a long syllable or two resolved syllables. See **Dip**.

Light verse: A verse with only one (primary) lift. See **Heavy verse** and **Normal verse.**

Linked alliteration: An intricate use of alliteration where the initial sound of the second lift in the off-verse anticipates the alliteration in the following line. See 2.2.2.

Long (or heavy) syllable: A syllable is long if it has a long vowel/diphthong or has a short vowel/diphthong closed by a consonant. Rhythmic stress normally falls on a long syllable.

Normal verse: A verse with two lifts. See **Heavy verse** and **Light verse.**

Off-verse: The second half of a line, also known as the b-verse or the second half-line.

On-verse: The first half of a line, also known as the a-verse or the first half-line.

Parasiting/parasitic/parasite: In the course of Old English, a word-final liquid or nasal became syllabic and a parasite vowel was inserted, as in *wundor* and *māðþum*. In Old English poetry, earlier nonparasiting forms like *wundr* and *māðþm* are often assumed for the sake of metre. See 4.2.2.

Particle: Particles lie midway between stress-words and proclitics: although not subordinated to any element, they do not have fully semantic force and hence usually fail to receive stress. If they are displaced from the first dip of a clause, however, particles bear rhythmic stress. Particles include finite verbs, demonstrative adverbs, personal pronouns, demonstrative pronouns, and some conjunctions.

Proclitic: Proclitics appear immediately before a stress-word so as to depend on it. They do not normally receive rhythmic stress unless they are displaced from their normal position before the noun. Proclitics comprise prepositions, demonstratives, possessives, copulative conjunctions (e.g., *ne*, *ond*), and prefixes.

Resolution: In Old English metre, a sequence of two syllables of which the first is short (i.e., ends with a short vowel or diphthong) is often regarded as equivalent to a single long syllable and thus may share rhythmic stress. The two resolved syllables are often joined with an arc.

Rhyme: End-rhyme plays a restricted role in Old English verse, usually serving as an optional embellishment to the verse-organizing alliteration. See 2.4.

Secondary stress: Secondary stress falls on the root syllable of the second compound element. See **Tertiary stress.**

Second half-line: See **Off-verse.**

Short (or light) syllable: A syllable is short if it ends with a short vowel or diphthong.

Stress-word: Stress-words are always rhythmically stressed, including nouns, adjectives, non-finite verbs (i.e., infinitives and participles), many adverbs, and some 'heavy' pronouns (e.g., *gehwylc, gehwæþer*).

Syncopation/syncopated: In Old English poetry, although they were syncopated or deleted in the poem as originally composed, short medial unstressed vowels are restored by the scribes. Such vowels can be ignored in scansion. See 4.2.3.

Tertiary stress: A type of secondary stress that can sometimes be metrically ignored. Constituents that bear tertiary stress are derivative suffixes such as *-ende, -en, -ra/-est, -ig, -ing, -līce, -nes, -sum,* and the penultimate syllable of Class II weak verbs. See 4.4.

Transverse alliteration: An ornate alliteration pattern where all four lifts in a line participate in alliteration in the pattern [AB: BA]. See 2.2.2.

Bibliography

Primary Sources

Alexander, Michael, ed. 2000. *Beowulf: A Glossed Text*. Rev. ed. Harmondsworth and New York: Penguin.

Bately, Janet M., ed. 1986. *The Anglo-Saxon Chronicle: A Collaborative Edition 3: MS. A*. Cambridge: D.S. Brewer.

Campbell, Alistair, ed. 1938. *The Battle of Brunanburh*. London: William Heinemann.

Chickering, Howell D., Jr, trans. and ed. 1977. *Beowulf: A Dual-Language Edition*. New York: Anchor Books.

Cook, Albert S., ed. 1889. *Judith: An Old English Epic Fragment*. 2nd ed., revised and enlarged. Boston: Heath.

– ed. 1900. *The Christ of Cynewulf*. Boston: Ginn.

– ed. 1919. *The Old English Elene, Phœnix, and Physiologus*. New Haven: Yale University Press.

Crépin, André, ed. 1991. *Beowulf*. 2 vols. Göppingen: Kümmerle.

Cubbin, G.P., ed. 1996. *The Anglo-Saxon Chronicle: A Collaborative Edition 6: MS D*. Cambridge: D.S. Brewer.

Fulk, R.D., Robert E. Bjork, and John D. Niles, eds. 2008. *Klaeber's Beowulf and the Fight at Finnsburg*. 4th ed. Toronto: University of Toronto Press. [Cited as Fulk, Bjork, and Niles]

Griffith, Mark, ed. 1997. *Judith*. Exeter: University of Exeter Press.

Heyne, Moritz, ed. 1963. *Beowulf*. 18th ed., revised by Else von Schaubert. Paderborn: F. Schöningh. [Cited as Heyne-von Schaubert]

Jack, George, ed. 1994. *Beowulf: A Student Edition*. Oxford: Clarendon Press.

Kent, Charles W., ed. 1889. *Elene: An Old English Poem*. Repr. New York: AMS Press, 1973.

Kiernan, Kevin, ed. 2004. *Electronic Beowulf*. 2.0. Digital Images of *Beowulf* Manuscript. Mac/Windows. London: The British Library.

Klaeber, Frederick, ed. 1950. *Beowulf and the Fight at Finnsburg*. 3rd ed. with 1st and 2nd Supplements. Lexington, MA: Heath. [Cited as Klaeber (3rd ed.)]

Krapp, George P., and Elliot V.K. Dobbie, eds. 1931–53. *The Anglo-Saxon Poetic Records*. 6 vols. New York: Columbia University Press. [Cited as Krapp-Dobbie]

Macrae-Gibson, O.D., ed. 1987. *The Old English Riming Poem*. Corrected reprint. Cambridge: D.S. Brewer.

Magoun, Francis P., Jr, ed. 1966. *Beowulf and Judith*, revised by Jess B. Bessinger, Jr. Cambridge, MA: Department of English, Harvard University.

Menner, Robert J., ed. 1941. *The Poetical Dialogues of Solomon and Saturn*. New York: Modern Language Association of America.

Mitchell, Bruce, and Fred C. Robinson, eds. 2006. *Beowulf: An Edition*. Rev. ed. Oxford: Blackwell. [Cited as Mitchell-Robinson]

Nickel, Gerhard, ed. 1976–82. *Beowulf und die kleineren Denkmäler der altenglischen Heldensage Waldere und Finnsburg*. 3 parts. Heidelberg: C. Winter.

Plummer, Charles, ed. 1892–9. *Two of the Saxon Chronicles Parallel*. 2 vols. Oxford: Clarendon Press. Repr. with a bibliographical note by Dorothy Whitelock, 1952.

Pope, John C., ed. 1967–8. *Homilies of Ælfric: A Supplementary Collection*. 2 vols. EETS o.s. 259, 260. London: Oxford University Press.

– ed. 2001. *Eight Old English Poems*. 3rd ed. revised by R.D. Fulk. New York and London: Norton. [Cited as Pope-Fulk]

Robinson, Fred C., and Eric G. Stanley, eds. 1991. *Old English Verse Texts from Many Sources*. Early English Manuscripts in Facsimile 23. Copenhagen: Rosenkilde and Bagger.

Scragg, D.G., ed. 1981. *The Battle of Maldon*. Manchester: Manchester University Press.

– ed. 1992. *The Vercelli Homilies and Related Texts*. EETS o.s. 300. Oxford: Oxford University Press.

Sedgefield, W.J., ed. 1910. *Beowulf*. Manchester: Manchester University Press. 2nd ed., 1913; 3rd ed., 1935.

– ed. 1968. *King Alfred's Old English Version of Boethius De Consolatione Philosophiae*. Repr. Darmstadt: Wisssenschaftliche Buchgesellschaft.

Slade, Benjamin, ed. 2002–3. *Beowulf on Steorarume* (*Beowulf in Cyberspace*). http://www.heorot.dk.

Swanton, Michael, ed. 1996. *The Dream of the Rood*. Exeter: University of Exeter Press.

– ed. 1997. *Beowulf*. Rev. ed. Manchester: Manchester University Press.

– trans. and ed. 2000. *The Anglo-Saxon Chronicles*. New ed. London: Phoenix.
Timmer, B.J., ed. 1978. *Judith*. Rev. ed. Exeter: University of Exeter.
Trask, Richard M., ed. 1997. *Beowulf and Judith: Two Heroes*. Lanham: University Press of America.
Wrenn, C.L., ed. 1996. *Beowulf with the Finnesburg Fragment*. Fully revised by W.F. Bolton. 5th ed. Exeter: University of Exeter Press. [Cited as Wrenn-Bolton]
Wyatt, A.J., ed. 1920. *Beowulf with the Finnsburg Fragment*. New ed. revised, with introduction and notes by R.W. Chambers. Repr. Cambridge: Cambridge University Press. [Cited as Wyatt-Chambers]

Secondary Sources

Ajiro, Atsushi. 2009. '*Beowulf* no Honbun wo Meguru Mondaiten to Sho-Kouteibon nitsuite' [Some Problems of the *Beowulf* Texts: With Reference to the Various Editions]. In *Essays on* Beowulf *and Other Medieval English Literature in Memory of Kinshiro Oshitari*, ed. Kazutomo Karasawa. Yokohama: Shumpusha, 389–408. [In Japanese]
Amos, Ashley C. 1980. *Linguistic Means of Determining the Dates of Old English Literary Texts*. Cambridge, MA: Medieval Academy of America.
Andrew, S.O. 1940. *Syntax and Style in Old English*. Cambridge: Cambridge University Press.
Baker, Peter S. 2007. *Introduction to Old English*. 2nd ed. Oxford: Blackwell.
Bammesberger, Alfred. 1980. 'Altenglische Komposita mit *hild(e)-*.' *Münchener Studien zur Sprachwissenschaft* 39: 5–10.
– 2001. 'Further Thoughts on *Beowulf*, Line 1537a: *Gefeng þa be [f]eaxe*.' *Notes and Queries* 48: 3–4.
Bessinger, J.B., Jr, ed. 1978. *A Concordance to the Anglo-Saxon Poetic Records*. Ithaca: Cornell University Press.
Blake, Norman F. 1977. 'The Dating of Old English Poetry.' In *An English Miscellany Presented to W.S. Mackie*, ed. Brian S. Lee. Cape Town: Oxford University Press, 14–27.
Bliss, A.J. 1962. *An Introduction to Old English Metre*. Oxford: Blackwell. Repr. with an introduction by Daniel Donoghue. Binghamton: Center for Medieval and Early Renaissance Studies, State University of New York (= Old English Newsletter Subsidia 20), 1993.
– 1967. *The Metre of* Beowulf. Rev. ed. Oxford: Blackwell.
– 1972. 'The Origin and Structure of the Old English Hypermetric Line.' *Notes and Queries* 19: 242–8.
– 1981. 'Auxiliary and Verbal in *Beowulf*.' *Anglo-Saxon England* 9: 157–82.

– 1995. *The Scansion of* Beowulf, ed. with a foreward by Peter J. Lucas. Old English Newsletter Subsidia 22. Kalamazoo: Medieval Institute, Western Michigan University and its Richard Rawlinson Center for Anglo-Saxon Studies.

Blockley, Mary. 2001. *Aspects of Old English Poetic Syntax: Where Clauses Begin.* Urbana: University of Illinois Press.

Blockley, Mary, and Thomas M. Cable. 1995. 'Kuhn's Laws, Old English Poetry, and the New Philology.' In Beowulf: *Basic Readings*, ed. Peter S. Baker. New York: Garland, 261–79.

Bosworth, Joseph, and T. Northcote Toller, eds. 1882–98. *An Anglo-Saxon Dictionary Based on the Manuscript Collections of the Late Joseph Bosworth.* Edited and enlarged by T. Northcote Toller. Repr. London: Oxford University Press, 1972. [Cited as Bosworth-Toller]

Bredehoft, Thomas A. 2003. 'Secondary Stress in Compound Germanic Nouns in Old English Verse.' *Journal of English Linguistics* 31: 199–220.

– 2004a. 'Ælfric and Late Old English Verse.' *Anglo-Saxon England* 33: 77–107.

– 2004b. 'The Boundaries Between Verse and Prose in Old English Literature.' In *Old English Literature in Its Manuscript Context*, ed. Joyce Tally Lionarons. Morgantown: West Virginia University Press, 139–72.

– 2005a. *Early English Metre*. Toronto: University of Toronto Press.

– 2005b. 'What Are Old English Metrical Studies For?' *Old English Newsletter* 39.1: 25–36.

– 2005c. 'Old English and Old Saxon Formulaic Rhyme.' *Anglia* 123: 204–29.

Brunner, Karl. 1951. *Altenglische Grammatik nach der angelsächsischen Grammatik von Eduard Sievers*. New ed. Halle: Max Niemeyer. [Cited as Sievers-Brunner]

Cable, Thomas. 1970. 'Rules for Syntax and Metrics in *Beowulf*.' *Journal of English and Germanic Philology* 69: 81–8.

– 1971a. 'Constraints on Anacrusis in Old English Meter.' *Modern Philology* 69: 97–104.

– 1971b. 'Clashing Stress in the Meter of *Beowulf*.' *Neuphilologische Mitteilungen* 72: 42–50.

– 1972. 'Metrical Simplicity and Sievers' Five Types.' *Studies in Philology* 69: 28–88.

– 1974. *The Meter and Melody of* Beowulf. Urbana: University of Illinois Press.

– 1981. 'Metrical Style as Evidence for the Date of *Beowulf*.' In *The Dating of* Beowulf, ed. Colin Chase. Toronto: University of Toronto Press and Centre for Medieval Studies, 77–82.

– 1984. 'Old English Prosody.' In *Approaches to Teaching* Beowulf, ed. Jess B. Bessinger, Jr and Robert F. Yeager. New York: Modern Language Association of America, 173–8.

– 1991. *The English Alliterative Tradition*. Philadelphia: University of Pennsylvania Press.

– 1993. 'Type D Verses as Evidence for the Rhythmic Basis of Old English Meter.' In *Heroic Poetry in the Anglo-Saxon Period: Studies in Honor of Jess B. Bessinger, Jr*, ed. Helen Damico and John Leyerle. Kalamazoo: Medieval Institute Publications, 157–70.

– 1994. 'Syllable Weight in Old English Meter: Grids, Morae, and Kaluza's Law.' *Diachronica* 11: 1–11.

– 2003. 'Kaluza's Law and the Progress of Old English Metrics.' In *Development in Prosodic Systems*, ed. Paula Fikkert and Haike Jacobs. Berlin: Mouton de Gruyter, 145–58.

Cain, Christopher M. 2001. 'Phonology and Meter in the Old English Macaronic Verses.' *Studies in Philology* 98: 273–91.

Campbell, Alistair. 1959. *Old English Grammar*. Oxford: Clarendon Press.

– 1970. 'Verse Influences in Old English Prose.' In *Philological Essays: Studies in Old and Middle English Language and Literature in Honour of Herbert Dean Meritt*, ed. James L. Rosier. The Hague and Paris: Mouton, 93–8.

Carroll, Benjamin H., Jr. 1993. 'Metrical Resolution in Old English.' *Journal of English and Germanic Philology* 92: 167–78.

Cassidy, Frederic G., and Richard N. Ringler, eds. 1971. *Bright's Old English Grammar and Reader*. 3rd ed., 2nd corrected printing. New York: Holt, Rinehart, and Winston.

Chase, Colin, ed. 1981. *The Dating of* Beowulf. Toronto: University of Toronto Press. Rev. ed., 1997.

Clemoes, Peter. 1966. 'Ælfric.' In *Continuations and Beginnings*, ed. Eric G. Stanley. London: Nelson, 176–209.

– 1995. *Interactions of Thought and Language in Old English Poetry*. Cambridge: Cambridge University Press.

Conner, Patrick W. 2001. 'On Dating Cynewulf.' In *The Cynewulf Reader*, ed. Robert E. Bjork. New York: Routledge, 23–56.

Cosmos, Spencer. 1976–7. 'Kuhn's Law and the Unstressed Verbs in *Beowulf*.' *Texas Studies in Literature and Language* 18: 306–28.

Creed, Robert P. 1966. 'A New Approach to the Rhythm of *Beowulf*.' *Publications of the Modern Language Association of America* 81: 23–33.

– 1982. 'The Basis of the Meter of *Beowulf*.' In *Approaches to Beowulfian Scansion*, Colloquium Series, no. 1, ed. Alain Renoir and Ann Hernandez. Berkeley: University of California, Department of English, 27–35.

– 1990. *Reconstructing the Rhythm of* Beowulf. Columbia: University of Missouri Press.

– 1993. 'Between the Lines: Subdominant-to-Dominant Patterning in *Beowulf*.' In *Heroic Poetry in the Anglo-Saxon Period: Studies in Honor of Jess B.*

Bessinger, Jr, ed. Helen Damico and John Leyerle. Kalamazoo: Medieval Institute Publications, 227–46.

Cronan, Dennis. 1986. 'Alliterative Rank in Old English Poetry.' *Studia Neophilologica* 58: 145–58.

– 2004. 'Poetic Words, Conservatism and the Dating of Old English Poetry.' *Anglo-Saxon England* 33: 23–50.

The Dictionary of Old English: A to G Online. Toronto: University of Toronto.

The Dictionary of Old English Web Corpus. Toronto: University of Toronto. [Cited as *DOE Web Corpus*]

Donoghue, Daniel. 1986. 'Word Order and Poetic Style: Auxiliary and Verbal in *The Metres of Boethius*.' *Anglo-Saxon England* 15: 167–96.

– 1987a. 'On the Classification of B-verses with Anacrusis in *Beowulf* and *Andreas*.' *Notes and Queries* 34: 1–5.

– 1987b. *Style in Old English Poetry: The Test of the Auxiliary*. New Haven: Yale University Press.

– 1990. 'Old English Meter.' *ANQ* (formerly published as *American Notes and Queries*) 3: 69–74.

– 1997. 'Language Matters.' In *Reading Old English Texts*, ed. Katherine O'Brien O'Keeffe. Cambridge: Cambridge University Press, 59–78.

– 2006. 'A Point Well Taken: Manuscript Punctuation and Old English Poems.' In *Inside Old English*, ed. John Walmsley. Oxford: Blackwell, 38–58.

Duggan, Hoyt N. 1988. 'The Evidential Basis for Old English Metrics.' *Studies in Philology* 85: 145–63.

Duncan, Edwin. 1985. 'Stress, Meter, and Alliteration in Old English Poetry.' PhD dissertation, University of Texas at Austin.

– 1986. 'Chronological Testing and the Scansion of *Frea* in Old English Poetry.' *Neuphilologische Mitteilungen* 87: 92–101.

– 1993. 'Weak Stress and Poetic Constraints in Old English Verse.' *Journal of English and Germanic Philology* 92: 495–508.

– 1994. 'Metrical and Alliterative Relationships in Old English and Old Saxon Verse.' *Studies in Philology* 91: 1–12.

Frank, Roberta. 2007. 'A Scandal in Toronto: *The Dating of* Beowulf a Quarter Century On.' *Speculum* 82: 843–64.

Fujiwara, Yasuaki. 1988. 'On the Function of Alliteration.' *English Linguistics* 5: 204–25.

– 1990. *Koeishi Inritsu Kenkyu* [Studies in Old English Metrics]. Hiroshima: Keisuisha. [In Japanese]

Fulk, R.D. 1989. 'West Germanic Parasiting, Sievers' Law, and the Dating of Old English Verse.' *Studies in Philology* 86: 117–38.

– 1990. 'Contraction as a Criterion for Dating Old English Verse.' *Journal of English and Germanic Philology* 89: 1–16.

– 1992. *A History of Old English Meter*. Philadelphia: University of Pennsylvania Press.

– 1997. 'Textual Criticism.' In *A* Beowulf *Handbook*, ed. Robert E. Bjork and John D. Niles. Lincoln: University of Nebraska Press, 35–54.

– 2001. 'Cynewulf: Canon, Dialect, and Date.' In *The Cynewulf Reader*, ed. Robert E. Bjork. New York: Routledge, 3–21.

– 2003. 'On Argumentation in Old English Philology, with Particular Reference to the Editing and Dating of *Beowulf*.' *Anglo-Saxon England* 32: 1–26.

– 2004. 'Old English Poetry and the Alliterative Revival: On Geoffrey Russom's "The Evolution of Middle English Alliterative Meter."' In *Studies in the History of the English Language II: Unfolding Conversations*, ed. Anne Curzan and Kimberly Emmons. Berlin: Mouton de Gruyter, 305–12.

– 2007a. 'Archaisms and Neologisms in the Language of *Beowulf*.' In *Studies in the History of the English Language III*, ed. Christopher M. Cain and Geoffrey Russom. Berlin: Mouton de Gruyter, 267–87.

– 2007b. 'Old English Meter and Oral Tradition: Three Issues Bearing on Poetic Chronology.' *Journal of English and Germanic Philology* 106: 304–24.

Gade, Kari Ellen, and R.D. Fulk. 2000. *A Bibliography of Germanic Alliterative Meters*. Old English Newsletter Subsidia 28. Kalamazoo: Medieval Institute, Western Michigan University.

Getty, Michael. 2002. *The Metre of* Beowulf: *A Constraint-Based Approach.* Berlin: Mouton de Gruyter.

Gneuss, Helmut. 1973. 'Guide to the Editing and Preparation of Texts for the *Dictionary of Old English*.' In *A Plan for the* Dictionary of Old English, ed. Roberta Frank and Angus Cameron. Toronto: University of Toronto Press, 9–24.

Golston, Chris, and Tomas Riad. 2003. 'Scansion and Alliteration in *Beowulf*.' *Jahrbuch für internationale Germanistik* 35: 77–105.

Grein, C.W.M., ed. 1861–4. *Sprachschatz der angelsächsischen Dichter*. Cassel and Göttingen: G.H. Wigand.

Griffith, M.S. 1991. 'Poetic Language and the Paris Psalter: The Decay of the Old English Tradition.' *Anglo-Saxon England* 20: 167–86.

– 2005. 'Verse Quite like *cwen to gebeddan* in *The Metres of Boethius*.' *Anglo-Saxon England* 34: 145–67.

Grinda, Klaus R. 1984. 'Pigeonholing Old English Poetry: Some Criteria of Metrical Style.' *Anglia* 102: 305–22.

Hall, J.R. Clark, trans. 1950. *Beowulf and the Finnesburg Fragment: A Translation into Modern English Prose*. New ed., completely revised with notes and an introduction by C.L. Wrenn, with prefatory remarks by J.R.R. Tolkien. London: George Allen and Unwin.

– ed. 1960. *A Concise Anglo-Saxon Dictionary*. 4th ed., with a supplement by Herbert D. Meritt. Cambridge: Cambridge University Press. Repr. Toronto: University of Toronto Press, 1984. [Cited as Clark Hall-Meritt]

Halle, Morris, and Samuel Jay Keyser. 1971. *English Stress: Its Form, Its Growth, and Its Role in Verse*. New York: Harper and Row.

Hazome, Takeichi, ed. 2005. *Koeishi Toin Jiten* [A Dictionary of Old English Alliteration]. Tokyo: Bunkashobo-hakubunsha. [In Japanese]

Healey, Antonette diPaolo, and Richard L. Venezky, eds. 1980. *A Microfiche Concordance to Old English*. Toronto: Centre for Medieval Studies, University of Toronto. [Cited as Healey-Venezky]

Heusler, Andreas. 1925. *Deutsche Versgeschichte, mit Einschluß des altenglischen und altnordischen Stabreimverses*. Berlin: W. de Gruyter.

– 1943. *Die altgermanische Dichtung*. 2nd ed. Potsdam: Athenaion.

Hieatt, Constance B. 1969. 'A New Theory of Triple Rhythm in the Hypermetric Lines of Old English Verse.' *Modern Philology* 67: 1–8.

– 1972. 'Prosodic Analysis of Old English Poetry: A Suggested Working Approach with Sample Applications.' *Revue de l'Université d' Ottawa* 42: 72–82.

– 1974. 'Alliterative Patterns in the Hypermetric Lines of Old English Verse.' *Modern Philology* 71: 237–42.

– 1980. '*Judith* and the Literary Function of Old English Hypermetric Lines.' *Studia Neophilologica* 52: 251–7.

Holthausen, Ferdinand. 1905. 'Beiträge zur Erklärung des altenglischen Epos.' *Zeitschrift für deutsche Philologie* 37: 113–25.

Hoops, Johannes. 1932. *Beowulfstudien*. Heidelberg: C. Winter.

Hoover, David L. 1985. *A New Theory of Old English Meter*. New York: Peter Lang.

Hutcheson, B.R. 1991. 'The Scansion of Old English Weak Verbs in *-ian*.' *Notes and Queries* 38: 144–6.

– 1992a. 'Accidental Alliteration in Old English Poetry: A Reconsideration.' *English Language Notes* 30: 1–10.

– 1992b. 'Kuhn's Law, Finite Verb Stress, and the Critics.' *Studia Neophilologica* 64: 129–39.

– 1993. 'Stress of Quantitative Adjectives and Some Common Adverbs in Old English Poetry: An Alternative to Kuhn's Laws.' *Leeds Studies in English* 24: 27–56.

– 1994. 'The Realizations of Tertiary Stress in Old English Poetry.' *Studies in Philology* 91: 13–34.

– 1995. *Old English Poetic Metre*. Cambridge: D.S. Brewer.

– 2004. 'Kaluza's Law, the Dating of *Beowulf*, and the Old English Poetic Tradition.' *Journal of English and Germanic Philology* 103: 297–322.

Irving, Edward B., Jr. 1998. 'Editing Old English Verse: The Ideal.' In *New Approaches to Editing Old English Verse*, ed. Sarah Larratt Keefer and Katherine O'Brien O'Keeffe. Cambridge: D.S. Brewer, 11–20.

Jack, George. 1999. 'Negative Contraction in Old English Verse.' *Review of English Studies* 50: 133–54.

Jakobson, Roman. 1963. 'On the So-Called Vowel Alliteration in Germanic Verse.' *Zeitschrift für Phonetik, Sprachwissenschaft und Kommunikationsforschung* 16: 85–92.

Kaluza, Max. 1894. *Der altenglische Vers: eine metrische Untersuchung, I: Kritik der bisherigen Theorien; II: Die Metrik des Beowulfliedes*. Berlin: Felber.

– 1896. 'Zur Betonungs- und Verslehre des Altenglischen.' In *Festschrift zum siebzigsten Geburtstage Oskar Schade.* Königsberg: Hartung, 101–33.

– 1909. *Englische Metrik in historischer Entwicklung.* Normannia: Germanische-romanische Bücherei, 1. Berlin: Emil Felber. [*A Short History of English Versification,* trans. A.C. Dunstan. London: George Allen, 1911.]

Keddie, James. 1995. 'Simplifying Resolution in *Beowulf*.' In *Prosody and Poetics in the Early Middle Ages: Essays in Honour of C.B. Hieatt*, ed. M.J. Toswell. Toronto: University of Toronto Press, 80–101.

Kendall, Calvin B. 1982. 'The Prefix *un*- and the Metrical Grammar of *Beowulf*.' *Anglo-Saxon England* 10: 39–52.

– 1983. 'The Metrical Grammar of *Beowulf*: Displacement.' *Speculum* 58: 1–30.

1991. *The Metrical Grammar of* Beowulf. Cambridge: Cambridge University Press.

Keyser, Samuel Jay. 1969a. 'Old English Prosody.' *College English* 30: 331–56.

– 1969b. 'Old English Prosody: A Demurrer: Reply.' *College English* 31: 74–80.

Kiernan, Kevin. 1996. Beowulf *and the* Beowulf *Manuscript*. Rev. ed. Ann Arbor: University of Michigan Press.

Kuhn, Hans. 1933. 'Zur Wortstellung und -betonung im Altgermanischen.' *Beiträge zur Geschichte der deutschen Sprache und Literatur* 57: 1–109. Repr. with an addendum in *Kleine Schriften*, ed. Dietrich Hofmann, vol. 1, 18–103. Berlin: W. de Gruyter, 1969.

Kuhn, Sherman M. 1973. 'Was Ælfric a Poet?' *Philological Quarterly* 52: 643–62.

Kuryłowicz, Jerzy. 1970. *Die sprachlichen Grundlagen der altgermanischen Metrik*. Innsbruck: Institut für vergleichende Sprachwissenschaft.

Lapidge, Michael. 1991. 'Textual Criticism and the Literature of Anglo-Saxon England.' *Bulletin of the John Rylands Library of Manchester* 73: 17–46.

– 1993. 'The Edition, Emendation and Reconstruction of Anglo-Saxon Texts.' In *The Politics of Editing Medieval Texts: Papers Given at the Twenty-Seventh*

Annual Conference on Editorial Problems, University of Toronto, 1–2 November 1991, ed. Roberta Frank. New York: AMS Press, 131–57.

– 1994. 'On the Emendation of Old English Texts.' In *The Editing of Old English: Papers from the 1990 Manchester Conference*, ed. D.G. Scragg and Paul E. Szarmach. Cambridge: D.S. Brewer, 53–67.

– 2000. 'The Archetype of *Beowulf*.' *Anglo-Saxon England* 29: 5–41.

– 2006. 'An Aspect of Old English Poetic Diction: The Postpositioning of Prepositions.' In *Inside Old English: Essays in Honour of Bruce Mitchell*, ed. John Walmsley. Oxford: Blackwell, 153–80.

Lehmann, W.P. 1968. 'Post-Consonantal *l m n r* and Metrical Practice in *Beowulf*.' In *Nordica et Anglica: Studies in Honor of Stefán Einarsson* (Janua Linguarum), ed. Allan H. Orrick. The Hague: Mouton, 148–67.

Lehmann, W.P., and Takemitsu Tabusa. 1958. *The Alliterations of the* Beowulf. Austin, Texas: Department of Germanic Languages, University of Texas at Austin.

Le Page, R.B. 1959. 'Alliterative Patterns as a Test of Style in Old English Poetry.' *Journal of English and Germanic Philology* 58: 434–41.

Lewis, Richard A. 1973. 'Alliteration and Old English Metre.' *Medium Ævum* 42: 119–30.

Lichtenheld, A. 1873. 'Das schwache Adjectiv im Angelsächsichen.' *Zeitschrift für deutsches Altertum* 16: 325–93.

Liuzza, Roy Michael. 1995. 'On the Dating of *Beowulf*.' In Beowulf: *Basic Readings*, ed. Peter S. Baker. New York: Garland, 281–302.

Lucas, Peter J. 1985. 'On Some Breaches of Kuhn's Law of Particles and *Genesis A* 2745.' *Philological Quarterly* 64: 386–91.

– 1987. 'Some Aspects of the Interaction between Verse Grammar and Metre in Old English Poetry.' *Studia Neophilologica* 59: 145–75.

Mackie, W.S. 1941. 'Notes upon the Text and Interpretation of *Beowulf*, II.' *Modern Language Review* 36: 95–8.

Macrae-Gibson, O.D. 1986. 'The Metrical Entities of Old English.' *Neuphilologische Mitteilungen* 87: 59–91.

Macrae-Gibson, O.D., and J.R. Lishman. 1998. 'Variety of Old English Metrical Usage.' *Neuphilologische Mitteilungen* 99: 139–71.

McCully, C.B., and J.J. Anderson, eds. 1996. *English Historical Metrics*. Cambridge: Cambridge University Press.

McCully, C.B., and Sharon Hilles. 2005. *The Earliest English: An Introduction to Old English Language*. Harlow: Pearson/Longman.

McIntosh, Angus. 1949. 'Wulfstan's Prose.' Sir Israel Gollancz Memorial Lecture for 1948. *Proceedings of the British Academy* 34: 109–42.

Mines, Rachel. 2002. 'An Examination of Kuhn's Second Law and Its Validity as a Metrical-Syntactical Rule.' *Studies in Philology* 99: 337–55.

Minkova, Donka. 1997. 'Velars and Palatals in Old English Alliteration.' In *Historical Linguistics 1997*, ed. Monika Schmid, Jennifer R. Austin, and Dieter Stein. Amsterdam: John Benjamins, 269–89.

– 2003. *Alliteration and Sound Change in Early English*. Cambridge: Cambridge University Press.

Minkova, Donka, and Robert P. Stockwell. 1994. 'Syllable Weight, Prosody, and Meter in Old English.' *Diachronica* 11: 35–64.

Mitchell, Bruce. 1969. 'Five Notes on Old English Syntax.' *Neuphilologische Mitteilungen* 70: 70–2.

– 1983. 'A Note on Negative Sentences in *Beowulf*.' *Poetica* 15–16: 9–12.

– 1985. *Old English Syntax*. 2 vols. Oxford: Clarendon.

– 2005. 'The Relationship between Old English Alliterative Verse and Ælfric's Alliterative Prose.' In *Latin Learning and English Lore: Studies in Anglo-Saxon Literature for Michael Lapidge*, ed. Katherine O'Brien O'Keeffe and Andy Orchard. Vol. 2. Toronto: University of Toronto Press, 349–62.

Mitchell, Bruce, and Fred C. Robinson, eds. 2007. *A Guide to Old English*. 7th edition. Oxford: Blackwell.

Momma, Haruko. 1996. 'Metrical Stress on Alliterating Finite Verbs in Clause-Initial *a*-verse: "Some Doubts and No Conclusions."' In *Studies in English Language and Literature. 'Doubt Wisely': Papers in Honour of E.G. Stanley*, ed. M.J. Toswell and E.M. Tyler. London and New York: Routledge, 186–98.

– 1997. *The Composition of Old English Poetry*. Cambridge: Cambridge University Press.

Nakagawa, Ryoichi. 1982. Beowulf *Kenkyu: Inritsu to Bunkozo* [A Study of *Beowulf*: Metre and Syntactic Structure]. Tokyo: Shohakusha. [In Japanese]

Neuner, Erich. 1920. 'Über ein- und dreihebige halbverse in der altenglischen alliterierenden poesie.' Inaugural-dissertation. Berlin.

Niles, John D. 1994. 'Editing *Beowulf*: What Can Study of the Ballads Tell Us?' *Oral Tradition* 9: 440-67.

Nist, John A. 1959. 'Alliterative Patterns in *Beowulf*: A Key to Authorship.' *Papers of the Michigan Academy of Science, Arts, and Letters* 44: 347–53.

– 1967. 'Metrical Uses of the Harp in *Beowulf*.' In *Old English Poetry: Fifteen Essays*, ed. Robert P. Creed. Providence: Brown University Press, 27–43.

Obst, Wolfgang. 1987. *Der Rhythmus des* Beowulf: *Eine Akzent- und Takttheorie.* Heidelberg: C. Winter.

Ogawa, Hiroshi. 2006. 'Koeishi *The Dream of the Rood* no Toingo to Toingata' [Alliterating Words and Types in the Old English Poem *The Dream of the Rood*]. In *Universals and Variation in Language* 1, The Center for Research on Language and Culture, Institute for Development of Social Intelligence, Senshu University, 39–42. [In Japanese]

Ogura, Michiko. 2009. 'A Non-metrical Approach to the Hypermetric Verses in *Beowulf*.' In *Essays on* Beowulf *and Other Medieval English Literature in Memory of Kinshiro Oshitari*, ed. Kazutomo Karasawa. Yokohama: Shumpusha, 267–77.

Orchard, Andy. 1995. 'Artful Alliteration in Anglo-Saxon Song and Story.' *Anglia* 113: 429–63.

Orton, Peter R. 1985. 'Verbal Apposition, Coordination and Metrical Stress in Old English.' *Neuphilologische Mitteilungen* 86: 145–58.

– 1999. 'Anglo-Saxon Attitudes to Kuhn's Laws.' *Review of English Studies* 50: 287–303.

Pope, John C. 1966. *The Rhythm of* Beowulf. Rev. ed. New Haven: Yale University Press.

– 1981. 'On the Date of Composition of *Beowulf*.' In *The Dating of* Beowulf, ed. Colin Chase. Toronto: University of Toronto Press and Centre for Medieval Studies, 187–95.

Quirk, Randolph. 1963. 'Poetic Language and Old English Metre.' In *Early English and Norse Studies: Presented to Hugh Smith in Honour of His Sixtieth Birthday*, ed. Arthur Brown and Peter Foole. London: Methuen, 150-71.

Raffel, Burton. 1975. '*Judith*: Hypermetricity and Rhetoric.' In *Anglo-Saxon Poetry: Essays in Appreciation for John C. McGalliard*, ed. Lewis E. Nicholson and Dolores Frese. Notre Dame, IN: University of Notre Dame Press, 124–34.

Richards, Mary P. 1992. 'Prosaic Poetry: Late Old English Poetic Composition.' In *Old English and New: Studies in Language and Linguistics in Honor of Frederic G. Cassidy*, ed. Joan H. Hall, Nick Doane, and Dick Ringler. Hamden, CT: Garland, 63–75.

Rieger, Max. 1876. 'Die alt- und angelsächsische Versekunst.' *Zeitschrift für deutsche Philologie* 7: 1–64.

Robinson, Fred C. 2008. 'The Anglo-Saxon Poetic Tradition.' In *A Companion to the History of the English Language*, ed. Haruko Momma and Michael Matto. Oxford: Wiley-Blackwell, 435–44.

Russom, Geoffrey. 1987. *Old English Meter and Linguistic Theory.* Cambridge: Cambridge University Press.

– 1995. 'Constraints on Resolution in *Beowulf*.' In *Prosody and Poetics in the Early Middle Ages: Essays in Honour of C.B. Hieatt*, ed. M.J. Toswell. Toronto: University of Toronto Press, 147–63.

– 1996. 'Purely Metrical Replacements for Kuhn's Laws.' In *English Historical Metrics*, ed. C.B. McCully and J.J. Anderson. Cambridge: Cambridge University Press, 30-41.

– 1998. Beowulf *and Old Germanic Metre*. Cambridge: Cambridge University Press.

– 2001. 'Metrical Evidence for Subordinate Stress in Old English.' *Journal of Germanic Linguistics* 13: 39–64.

– 2002a. 'A Bard's-eye View of the Germanic Syllable.' *Journal of English and Germanic Philology* 101: 305–28.

– 2002b. 'Dating Criteria for Old English Poems.' In *Studies in the History of the English Language: A Millennial Perspective,* ed. Donka Minkova and Robert Stockwell. Berlin: Mouton de Gruyter, 245–65.

– 2007. 'Evolution of the A-verse in English Alliterative Meter.' In *Studies in the History of the English Language III*, ed. Christopher M. Cain and Geoffrey Russom. Berlin: Mouton de Gruyter, 63–87.

– 2008. 'History of English Prosody.' In *A Companion to the History of the English Language*, ed. Haruko Momma and Michael Matto. Oxford: Wiley-Blackwell, 81–7.

Sarrazin, Gregor. 1907. 'Zur Chronologie und Verfasserfrage angelsächsischer Dichtungen.' *Englische Studien* 38: 145–95.

Sato, Kiriko. 2002. 'Case-forms and *mid*-Phrases in the Old English *Metres of Boethius*: A Comparison with the Prose Version.' *Studies in Medieval English Language and Literature* 17: 41–58.

Schwetman, John W. 1993. 'An Assessment of Kuhn's Laws of Stress in Old English Poetry.' *Neuphilologische Mitteilungen* 94: 47–60.

Sievers, Eduard. 1885. 'Zur Rhythmik des germanischen Alliterationsverses.' *Beiträge zur Geschichte der deutschen Sprache und Literatur* 10: 209–314, 451–545.

– 1893. *Altgermanische Metrik*. Halle: Max Niemeyer.

Sisam, Kenneth. 1946. 'Notes on Old English Poetry.' *Review of English Studies* 22: 257–68.

– 1953. *Studies in the History of Old English Literature*. Oxford: Clarendon Press.

Sledd, James. 1969. 'Old English Prosody: A Demurrer.' *College English* 31: 71–4.

Sohn, Chang-Yong. 1996. 'The Metrical Structure of *Beowulf*.' PhD dissertation, Stanford University.

Stanley, Eric G. 1963. Review of *The Metre of* Beowulf, by A.J. Bliss. *English Philological Studies* 8: 47–53.

– 1971. 'Studies in the Prosaic Vocabulary of Old English Verse.' *Neuphilologische Mitteilungen* 72: 385–418.

– 1974. 'Some Observations on the A3 Lines in *Beowulf*.' In *Old English Studies in Honour of John C. Pope*, ed. Robert B. Burlin and Edward B. Irving, Jr. Toronto: University of Toronto Press, 139–64.

– 1975. 'Verbal Stress in Old English Verse.' *Anglia* 93: 307–34.

– 1981. 'The Date of *Beowulf*: Some Doubts and No Conclusions.' In *The Dating of* Beowulf, ed. Colin Chase. Toronto: University of Toronto Press and Centre for Medieval Studies, 197–211.

– 1984. 'Unideal Principles of Editing Old English Verse.' *Proceedings of the British Academy* 70: 231–73.

– 1985. '*The Judgement of the Damned* (from Cambridge, Corpus Christi College 201 and Other Manuscripts), and the Definition of Old English Verse.' In *Learning and Literature in Anglo-Saxon England: Studies Presented to Peter Clemoes on the Occasion of His Sixty-fifth Birthday*, ed. Michael Lapidge and Helmut Gneuss. Cambridge: Cambridge University Press, 363–91. Repr. with improvements in Stanley (1987: 352–83).

– 1987. *A Collection of Papers with Emphasis on Old English Literature*. Toronto: Pontifical Institute of Mediaeval Studies.

– 1988. 'Rhymes in English Medieval Verse: from Old English to Middle English.' In *Medieval English Studies Presented to George Kane*, ed. Edward Donald Kennedy, Ronald Waldron, and Joseph S. Wittig. Wolfeboro: D.S. Brewer, 19–54.

– 1992. 'Initial Clusters of Unstressed Syllables in Half-lines of *Beowulf*.' In *Words, Texts and Manuscripts: Studies in Anglo-Saxon Culture Presented to Helmut Gneuss*, ed. Michael Korhammer. Cambridge: D.S. Brewer, 263–84.

– 1994. *In the Foreground:* Beowulf. Woodbridge, Suffolk: D.S. Brewer.

– 1999. 'Transverse Alliteration.' *Notes and Queries* 46: 484.

Stevick, R.D. 1968. *Suprasegmentals, Meter, and the Manuscript of* Beowulf. The Hague: Mouton.

Stockwell, Robert P. 1996. 'On Recent Theories of Metrics and Rhythm in *Beowulf*.' In *English Historical Metrics*, ed. C.B. McCully and J.J. Anderson. Cambridge: Cambridge University Press, 73–94.

Stockwell, Robert P., and Donka Minkova. 1992. 'Kuhn's Laws and Verb-Second: On Kendall's Theory of Syntactic Displacement in *Beowulf*.' In *On Germanic Linguistics: Issues and Methods*, ed. Irmengard Rauch, Gerald F. Carr, and Robert L. Kyes. Berlin and New York: Mouton de Gruyter, 315–37.

– 1994. 'Kuhn's Laws and the Rise of Verb-Second Syntax.' In *Language Change and Language Structure: Older Germanic Languages in a Comparative Perspective*, ed. Toril Swan, Endre Mørck, and Olaf Jansen Westwik. Berlin: Mouton de Gruyter, 213–31.

– 1995. 'Against the Notion "Metrical Grammar."' In *Insights in Germanic Linguistics II: Classic and Contemporary,* ed. Irmengard Rauch and Gerald F. Carr. Berlin and New York: Mouton de Gruyter, 243–55.

– 1997a. 'Prosody.' In *A* Beowulf *Handbook*, ed. Robert E. Bjork and John D. Niles. Lincoln: University of Nebraska Press, 55–83.

– 1997b. 'Old English Metrics and the Phonology of Resolution.' In *Germanic Studies in Honor of Anatoly Liberman, NOWELE* 31–2*:* 389–406.

Suzuki, Seiichi. 1994. 'On the Combination of Type A Verses into Lines in *Beowulf*: A Further Consideration.' *Notes and Queries* 41: 437–9.

– 1995a. 'Resolution and Mora Counting in Old English.' *American Journal of Germanic Linguistics and Literature* 7: 1–28.
– 1995b. 'In Defense of Resolution as a Metrical Principle in the Meter of *Beowulf*.' *English Studies* 76: 20–33.
– 1995c. 'Anacrusis in the Meter of *Beowulf*.' *Studies in Philology* 92: 141–63.
– 1996a. *The Metrical Organization of* Beowulf: *Prototype and Isomorphism*. Berlin: Mouton de Gruyter.
– 1996b. 'Preference Conditions for Resolution in the Meter of *Beowulf*: Kaluza's Law Reconsidered.' *Modern Philology* 93: 281–306.
– 2004. *The Metre of Old Saxon Poetry: The Remaking of Alliterative Tradition*. Cambridge: D.S. Brewer.
Suzuki, Yasuko. 2008. 'Finite Verb Stress and Clitic Verbs in Old English *Beowulf*.' PhD dissertation, University of Illinois at Urbana-Champaign.
Terasawa, Jun. 1989. 'Metrical Constraints on Old English Compounds.' *Poetica* 31: 1–16.
– 1992. 'Old English *here-toga* and Its Germanic Equivalents: A Metrical and Lexical Study.' *Studies in Medieval English Language and Literature* 7: 35–51.
– 1994. *Nominal Compounds in Old English: A Metrical Approach*. Copenhagen: Rosenkilde and Bagger.
– 1995. 'The *Helle* Sequence in Old English Poetry: A Compound or a Syntactic Phrase?' In *Essays in Linguistics and Philology Presented to Professor Kinsuke Hasegawa on the Occasion of His Sixtieth Birthday*, ed. Akira Baba. Tokyo: Kenkyusha, 615–27.
– 1998. 'The *Helle* Sequence in Old English Poetry Revisited.' In *English Historical Linguistics and Philology in Japan*, ed. Jacek Fisiak and Akio Oizumi. Berlin: Mouton de Gruyter, 387–99.
– 2001. 'The Scarcity of Formations in *-ere* in Old English Poetry.' *Anglia* 119: 193–206.
– 2005. 'Negative Constructions in Old English: The Question of Cynewulf's Authorship.' In *Aspects of English Negation*, ed. Yoko Iyeiri. Amsterdam: John Benjamins, 15–25.
– 2007a. 'Agent-Nouns in *-end*: The Use of Alternative Plurals as Metrical Variants in Old English Poetry.' In *Language and Beyond: A Festschrift for Hiroshi Yonekura on the Occasion of His 65th Birthday*, ed. Mayumi Sawada, Larry Walker, and Shizuya Tara. Tokyo: Eichosha, 491–507.
– 2007b. 'Is Beowulf a Spy? A Note on *Beowulf* 253a.' In *Text, Language and Interpretation: Essays in Honour of Keiko Ikegami*, ed. Yoshiyuki Nakao, Shoko Ono, Naoko Shirai, Kaoru Noji, and Masahiko Kanno. Tokyo: Eihosha, 79–91.
– 2009. '*Beowulf* niokeru 3 onsetsu ika hangyo nitsuite' [Notes on Half-lines of Three or Fewer Syllables in *Beowulf*]. In *Essays on* Beowulf *and Other*

Medieval English Literature in Memory of Kinshiro Oshitari, ed. Kazutomo Karasawa. Yokohama: Shumpusha, 278–93. [In Japanese]

– 2010. 'The Weak Man in Old English Poetry.' *Journal of English and Germanic Philology* 109: 22–32.

Timmer, B.J. 1952. 'Expanded Lines in Old English Poetry.' *Neophilologus* 35: 226–30.

Toswell, M.J., ed. 1995. *Prosody and Poetics in the Early Middle Ages: Essays in Honour of C.B. Hieatt*. Toronto: University of Toronto Press.

Townsend, Julie. 1996. 'The Metre of the *Chronicle*-Verse.' *Studia Neophilologica* 68: 143–76.

Vickman, Jeffrey. 1990. *A Metrical Concordance to* Beowulf. With a preface by R.D. Fulk. Binghamton: Center for Medieval and Early Renaissance Studies, State University of New York at Binghamton.

Weyhe, Hans. 1905. 'Beiträge zur westgermanischen Grammatik.' *Beiträge zur Geschichte der deutschen Sprache und Literatur* 30: 55–141.

Whitman, F.H. 1993. *A Comparative Study of Old English Metre.* Toronto: University of Toronto Press.

Willard, Rudolph, and Elinor D. Clemons. 1967. 'Bliss's Light Verses in the *Beowulf*.' *Journal of English and Germanic Philology* 66: 230–44.

Yakovlev, Nicolay. 2008. 'The Development of Alliterative Metre from Old to Middle English.' PhD dissertation, University of Oxford.

Yamanouchi, Kazuyoshi. 1984. '*Beowulf* niokeru Hitoin Doshi' [Some Notes on Non-alliterating Finite Verbs in *Beowulf*]. In *Studies in English Philology and Linguistics in Honour of Dr. Tamotsu Matsunami*, ed. Shigeru Ono. Tokyo: Shubun International, 65–80. [In Japanese]

– 1986. 'Toin *sc* to *The Paris Psalter*' [*SC* Alliteration in the Metrical Version of the *Paris Psalter*]. *Jinbun Ronshu* 36 (Shizuoka University): 59–88. [In Japanese]

Yoshino, Yoshihiro. 1978. 'Koeigo no Hitei nitsuite – Sanbun to Shi no Hikaku, I' [Some Neglected Aspects of Negation in Old English: A Comparison between Verse and Prose]. *Ronso: Bulletin of the Faculty of Letters* 18 (Tamagawa University): 75–106. [In Japanese]

– 1984. 'Poetic Syntax in the Old English *Meters of Boethius*: A Comparative Study of Verse and Prose.' PhD dissertation, University of Pennsylvania.

Zehnder, Ursula. 2000. 'Hypermetrical Verse Patterns in the Riddles of the Exeter Book.' *Notes and Queries* 47: 405–9.

– 2001. 'A Metrical Comparison of *Beowulf* and the *Old English Riddles* of the Exeter Book.' In *Authors, Heroes and Lovers: Essays on Medieval English Literature and Language*, ed. Thomas Honegger. Bern: Peter Lang, 27–46.

Index of Verses

This index includes all verses and lines that are quoted for discussion in the text, exercises, and notes. It does not list verses and lines that are cited just by number or those cited in the appendices. Verse and line numbers are in bold and italics followed by a colon; the number after the colon indicates the page or pages on which the verse/line is quoted.

General Index

This index is not exhaustive but refers to definitions and to principal discussions of the term in question. Those terms referred to in the appendices are not included.

Toronto Anglo-Saxon Series

1 *Preaching the Converted: The Style and Rhetoric of the Vercelli Book Homilies*, Samantha Zacher

2 *Say What I Am Called: The Old English Riddles of the Exeter Book and the Anglo-Latin Riddle Tradition*, Dieter Bitterli

3 *The Aesthetics of Nostalgia: Historical Representation in Anglo-Saxon Verse*, Renée Trilling

4 *New Readings in the Vercelli Book*, edited by Samantha Zacher and Andy Orchard

5 *Authors, Audiences, and Old English Verse*, Thomas A. Bredehoft

6 *On the Aesthetics of* Beowulf *and Other Old English Poems*, edited by John M. Hill

7 *Old English Metre: An Introduction*, Jun Terasawa